DISCARDED

STUDY GUIDE for DISCOVERING COMPUTERS 2000

Concepts for a Connected World

Web and CNN Turner Learning Enhanced

Gary B. Shelly
Thomas J. Cashman
Tim J. Walker

COURSE TECHNOLOGY
ONE MAIN STREET
CAMBRIDGE MA 02142
Thomson Learning™

SHELLY
CASHMAN
SERIES®

COPYRIGHT © 2000 Course Technology, a division of Thomson Learning.
Thomson Learning is a trademark used herein under license.

Printed in the United States of America

For more information, contact:

Course Technology
One Main Street
Cambridge, Massachusetts 02142, USA

or find us on the World Wide Web at: www.course.com

Asia (excluding Japan)
Thomson Learning
60 Albert Street, #15-01
Albert Complex
Singapore 189969

Japan
Thomson Learning
Palaceside Building 5F
1-1-1 Hitotsubashi, Chiyoda-ku
Tokyo 100 0003 Japan

Australia/New Zealand
Nelson/Thomson Learning
102 Dodds Street
South Melbourne, Victoria 3205
Australia

Latin America
Thomson Learning
Seneca, 53
Colonia Polanco
11560 Mexico D.F. Mexico

South Africa
Thomson Learning
Zonnebloem Building,
Constantia Square
526 Sixteenth Road
P.O. Box 2459
Halfway House, 1685
South Africa

Canada
Nelson/Thomson Learning
1120 Birchmount Road
Scarborough, Ontario
Canada M1K 5G4

UK/Europe/Middle East
Thomson Learning
Berkshire House
168-173 High Holborn
London, WC1V 7AA United Kingdom

Spain
Thomson Learning
Calle Magallanes, 25
28015-MADRID
ESPANA

ALL RIGHTS RESERVED. No part of this work may be reproduced, transcribed, or used in any form or by any means–graphic, electronic, or mechanical, including photocopying, recording, taping, Web distribution or information storage and retrieval systems–without the prior written permission of the publisher.

For permission to use material from this text or product, contact us by
- Web: www.thomsonrights.com
- Phone: 1-800-730-2214
- Fax: 1-800-730-2215

TRADEMARKS
Course Technology and the Open Book logo are registered trademarks and CourseKits is a trademark of Course Technology.

SHELLY CASHMAN SERIES® and **Custom Edition**® are trademarks of Thomson Learning. Some of the product names and company names used in this book have been used for identification purposes only and may be trademarks or registered trademarks of their respective manufacturers and sellers. Thomson Learning and Course Technology disclaim any affiliation, association, or connection with, or sponsorship or endorsement by, such owners.

DISCLAIMER
Course Technology reserves the right to revise this publication and make changes from time to time in its content without notice.

ISBN 0-7895-4633-7

1 2 3 4 5 6 7 8 9 10 BC 04 03 02 01 00

DISCOVERING COMPUTERS 2000
CONCEPTS FOR A CONNECTED WORLD
STUDY GUIDE

CONTENTS

PREFACE

This *Study Guide* is intended as a supplement to *Discovering Computers 2000: Concepts for a Connected World, Web and CNN Enhanced.* A variety of learning activities are provided in a format that is easy to follow and helps students recall, review, and master introductory computer concepts. Each chapter in the *Study Guide* includes:

- A **Chapter Overview** summarizing the chapter's content that helps students recollect the general character of the concepts presented.
- **Chapter Objectives** specifying the goals students should have achieved after finishing the chapter.
- A **Chapter Outline** designed to be completed by the students, helping them to identify, organize, and recognize the relationships between important concepts.
- A **Self Test** that reviews the material in the chapter through Matching, True/False, Multiple Choice, Fill in the Blanks, and Complete the Table questions.
- Questions suggesting **Things to Think About**, formulated to help students develop a deeper understanding of the information in the chapter.
- A **Puzzle** that provides an entertaining approach to reviewing important terms and concepts.
- **Self Test Answers** and a **Puzzle Answer** that students can use to assess their mastery of the subject matter.

In addition to the activities in each chapter, the *Study Guide* also offers a **To the Student** section that provides tips on using the textbook effectively, attending class, preparing for and taking tests, and using this *Study Guide*.

Acknowledgments

The Shelly Cashman Series would not be the leading computer education series without the contributions of outstanding publishing professionals. First, and foremost, among them is Becky Herrington, director of production and designer. She is the heart and soul of the Shelly Cashman series, and it is only through her leadership, dedication, and tireless efforts that superior products are made possible. Becky created and produced the award-winning Windows series of books.

Under Becky's direction, the following individuals made significant contributions to these books: Doug Cowley, production manager; Ginny Harvey, series specialist and developmental editor; Ken Russo, senior Web designer; Mark Norton, Web Designer; Mike Bodnar, associate production manager; Stephanie Nance, graphic artist and cover designer; Jeanne Black and Betty Hopkins, Quark experts; and Margaret Gatling, proofreader.

Special thanks go to Richard Keaveny, managing editor; Jim Quasney, series consultant; Lora Wade, product manager; Meagan Walsh, associate product manager; Francis Schurgot, Web product manager; Scott Wiseman, online developer; Rajika Gupta, marketing manager; and Erin Bennett, editorial assistant.

Gary B. Shelly
Thomas J. Cashman
Timothy J. Walker

TO THE STUDENT

Would you like to be promised success in this course? Your textbook, *Discovering Computers 2000*, can be a source of the knowledge you will need to excel. Unfortunately, no textbook alone can guarantee mastery of the subject matter; genuine understanding depends to a great extent on how hard you are willing to work. Other available resources, however, can *help* you to get the most out of this course. That is the intent of this Study Guide.

What follows are tips on using the textbook, attending class, preparing for and taking tests, and utilizing this Study Guide. Most of the tips in the first three areas not only will help to improve your performance in this course, they also can be applied to many of your other college classes. The tips in the last area are designed to explain how this Study Guide can enhance your understanding of the material in *Discovering Computers 2000.*

🕮 Using the Textbook

The textbook is one of your most important tools for building a solid foundation in the subject matter. To use your textbook most effectively, follow these guidelines:

Survey the whole text first. The preface explains the authors' goals, objectives, point of view, assumptions, and instructional approach. The table of contents supplies an overview of the topics covered. Notice how chapters are organized, the way key terms and concepts are indicated, how illustrations and tables are used, and the types of exercises that conclude each chapter. Look for special features interspersed throughout the book and use the index to clarify information.

Start by skimming the chapter. Read the chapter introduction, which gives you a general idea of the chapter's content, and study the chapter objectives, which indicate what you are expected to learn. Next, browse the chapter. Look at the section headings to get a feeling for how sections are related to each other. Notice bold or italic text; usually, these words are important. Finally, read the In Brief summary at the end of the chapter. The summary will restate, in broad terms, the major concepts and conclusions offered in the chapter.

Carefully read the entire chapter. Some instructors prefer that you only skim a chapter before class, and then do a detailed reading after their lecture. Other instructors want you to read the chapter thoroughly before class. Whenever you sit down to read the entire chapter, first review the exercises at the end of the chapter to provide a more specific focus for your reading. As you read through the text, make sure you understand all of the key terms and concepts. Pay particular attention to illustrations (photographs, diagrams, and tables) and their captions; often, they can help clarify ideas in the text. Write in your book: highlight important points, note relationships, and jot questions. Read the Technology Trailblazer and Company on the Cutting Edge sections that conclude each chapter in *Discovering Computers 2000.* These sections highlight people and corporations that have made significant contributions to the computer industry. Carefully examine the summary material (In Brief) and list of important words (Key Terms). If there is anything you do not remember or understand, go back and re-read the relevant sections. Do the exercises that deal specifically with the content of the chapter (Checkpoint). Finally, complete any additional exercises (At the Movies, At Issue, CyberClass, Hands On, Net Stuff) that your instructor may assign.

Attending Class

Attending class is a key ingredient to success in a course. Simply showing up, however, is not enough. To get the most out of class, follow these guidelines:

Arrive early and prepared. Sit close enough to the front of the room to hear well and see any visual materials, such as transparencies, clearly. Have any necessary supplies, such as a notebook and writing implement or a laptop computer, and your textbook. Be ready to start when your instructor begins.

Take notes. For most people, taking notes is essential to later recall the material presented in class. Note taking styles vary: some people simply jot down key words and concepts, while others prefer to write more detailed accounts. The important thing is that the style you adopt works for you. If, when you later consult your notes, you find they do little to help you remember the subject of the lecture, perhaps you should try to be more comprehensive. If you find that in taking notes you frequently fall behind your instructor, try to be briefer. Review your notes as soon as possible after class, while the material is still fresh.

Do not hesitate to ask questions. Often, people are afraid to ask questions because they think they will appear foolish. In reality, asking good questions is a sign of intelligence; after all, you have to be insightful enough to realize something is unclear. Keep in mind that often your classmates have the same questions you do. Good questions not only help to clarify difficult topics, they also increase the depth of your understanding by suggesting relationships between ideas or establishing the significance of concepts. Learn the best time to ask questions. In small classes, sometimes it is possible to ask questions during instruction. In a larger setting, it may be best to approach your instructor after class or to make an appointment. If you feel really lost, your instructor may be able to recommend a peer tutor or an academic counseling service to help you.

Preparing for and Taking Tests

Tests are an opportunity for you to demonstrate how much you have learned. Some strategies are certain to improve performance on tests. To do your best on a test, follow these guidelines:

Find out as much as you can about the test. Ask your instructor what material will be covered, what types of questions will be used, how much time you will have, and what supplies you will need (pencil or pen, paper or bluebook, perhaps even notes or a textbook if it is an open-book test). You will be more likely to do your best work if there are no surprises. Occasionally, copies of previous tests are available from the department or school library. These are invaluable aids in test preparation.

Use your resources wisely. Start studying by reviewing your notes and, in *Discovering Computers 2000*, the In Brief section at the end of each chapter. Review carefully and attempt to anticipate some of the questions that may be asked. Re-read the sections in your textbook on topics you are not sure of or that seem especially important. Try to really comprehend, and not merely memorize, the material. If you truly understand a concept, you will be able to answer any question, no matter what type or how it is worded. Understanding often makes remembering easier, too; for example, if you know how an ink-jet printer works, it is simple to recall that ink-jet printer resolution is measured in dots per inch (dpi). When memorizing is necessary, use whatever technique works (memory tricks, verbal repetition, flash cards, and so on).

Avoid cramming. To prepare for an athletic contest, you would not practice for twelve straight hours before the event. In the same way, you should not expect to do well on a test by spending the entire night before it cramming. When you cram, facts become easily confused, and anything you do keep straight probably will be remembered only for a short time. It also is difficult to recognize how concepts are related, which can be an important factor in successful test taking. Try to study in increments over a period of time. Use the night before the test to do a general review of the pertinent material, concentrating on what seems most difficult. Then, get a good night's sleep so you are well rested and at your best when it is time for the test.

Take time to look through the test. Arrive early enough at the test site to get properly settled. Listen for any special instructions that might be given. Skim the entire test before you start. Read the directions carefully; you may not have to answer every question, or you may be asked to answer questions in a certain way. Determine the worth of each part, the parts you think can be done most quickly, and the parts you believe will take the longest to complete. Use your assessment to budget your time.

Answer the questions you are sure of first. As you work through the test, read each question carefully and answer the easier ones first. If you are not certain of an answer, skip that question for now, ensuring you get the maximum number of "sure" points and reducing worry about time when later dealing with the more difficult questions. Occasionally, you will find that the information you needed to answer one of the questions you skipped can be found elsewhere in the test. Other times, you will suddenly remember what you need to answer a question you skipped as you are dealing with another part of the test.

Use common sense. Most questions have logical answers. While these answers often require specific knowledge of the subject matter, sometimes it is possible to determine a correct answer with a general understanding and a little common sense. As you work through a test, and when you go back over the test after you are finished, make sure all your answers are reasonable. Do not change an answer, however, unless you are sure your first answer was wrong. If incorrect answers are not penalized any more than having no answer at all, it is better to try a logical guess than to leave an answer blank.

But, if you are penalized for incorrect answers (for example, if your final score is the number of correct answers minus the number of incorrect answers), you will have to decide whether or not to answer a question based on how confident you are of your guess.

✎ Using this Study Guide

The purpose of this Study Guide is to further your understanding of the concepts presented in *Discovering Computers 2000*. The Study Guide chapter should be completed *after* you have finished the corresponding chapter in the book. The Study Guide chapters are divided into sections, each of which has a specific purpose:

Chapter Overview This is a brief summary of the chapter's content. The Chapter Overview helps you recall the general nature of the information in the chapter.

Chapter Objectives This is a roster of the same objectives that introduce the chapter in the book. After completing the chapter, review the Chapter Objectives to determine how many of them you have met. If you have not reached an objective, go back and review the appropriate material or your notes.

Chapter Outline This is a partially completed outline of the chapter with page numbers where topics can be found. The Chapter Outline is designed to help you review the material and to assist you in organizing and seeing the relationships between concepts. Complete the outline in as much depth as you feel necessary. You can refer directly to the text as you work through the outline while re-reading the chapter, or you can fill in the outline on your own and then use the text to check the information you have supplied.

Self Test This is a tool you can use to evaluate your mastery of the chapter. The Self Test consists of five different types of questions: matching, true/false, multiple choice, fill in the blanks, and complete the table. Take the test without referring to your textbook or notes. Leave any answer you are unsure of blank or, if you prefer, guess at the answer but indicate you were unsure by placing a question mark (?) after your response. When you have finished, check your work against the answers at the end of the Study Guide chapter. Each answer is accompanied by the page number in *Discovering Computers 2000* where the answer can be found. Review any solution that was incorrect or any reply that was uncertain.

Things to Think About These questions are meant to help you better grasp the information in each chapter. Because specific answers to the Things to Think About questions will vary, no solutions are given. The true purpose of these questions is to get you to contemplate the "why" behind concepts, thus encouraging you to gain a greater understanding of the ideas, their connections, and their significance.

Puzzle This activity is designed to review important terms in an entertaining fashion. The Puzzle in each chapter is one of four types: a word search puzzle, a crossword puzzle, a puzzle in which words must be placed in a grid, or a puzzle involving words written in code. Every puzzle offers definitions or descriptions and asks you to supply the associated term. The solution to each puzzle is given.

DISCOVERING COMPUTERS 2000

STUDY GUIDE

CHAPTER 1

Introduction to Using Computers

Chapter Overview

This chapter presents a broad survey of concepts and terminology related to computers. The idea of computer literacy is introduced. You discover what a computer is and what it does. You learn about the components of a computer, the power of computers, computer software, and networks and the Internet. Categories of computers are identified, including personal computers, minicomputers, mainframe computers, and supercomputers. Finally, you find out how people employ computers, from home users to large business users. Reading and understanding the material in this chapter should help you to better understand these topics as they are presented in more detail in the following chapters.

Chapter Objectives

After completing this chapter, you should be able to:

- Explain why it is important to be computer literate
- Define the term computer
- Identify the components of a computer
- Explain why a computer is a powerful tool
- Differentiate among the various categories of software
- Explain the purpose of a network
- Discuss the uses of the Internet and the World Wide Web
- Describe the categories of computers and their uses

Chapter Outline

I. Computer literacy [p. 1.2]

Computer literacy is a knowledge and understanding of computers and their uses.

II. What is a computer and what does it do? [p. 1.3]

A computer is ____

____

____

- Data is ____
- Information is ____

Computers manipulate and process data (*input*) to create information (*output*) and can hold data and information for future use in an area called storage.

The information processing cycle is the cycle of ______________________________

____

III. The components of a computer [p. 1.5]

Hardware is the electric, electronic, and mechanical equipment that makes up a computer. A computer consists of a variety of hardware components.

A. Input devices [p. 1.5]

An input device allows ______________________________

____

Common input devices: ______________________________

B. Output devices [p. 1.6]

An output device is used to ______________________________

____

Common output devices: ______________________________

C. System unit [p. 1.6]

The system unit is ______________________________

____

The central processing unit (CPU) is ______________________________

____

Memory is ______________________________

____

D. Storage devices [p. 1.7]

A storage medium is ______________________________

____

A storage device is used to ______________________________

____

Common storage devices: ______________________________

E. Communications devices [p. 1.8]

Communications devices enable ______________________________

____

IV. Why is a computer so powerful? [p. 1.8]

A computer's power is derived from its:

A. Speed [p. 1.8]

____

B. Reliability [p. 1.8]

____

C. Accuracy [p. 1.8]

____

D. Storage [p. 1.8]

____

E. Communications [p. 1.8]

____

V. Computer software [p. 1.9]

A computer program is ______________________________

____

A. System software [p. 1.10]

System software consists of ______________________________

____

1. Operating system [p. 1.10]

The operating system contains ______________________________

____

2. Utility programs [p. 1.11]

Utility programs perform ______________________________

____

3. User interface [p. 1.11]

A user interface is ______________________________

____

A graphical user interface (GUI) allows ______________________________

____

B. Application software [p. 1.12]

Application software consists of ______________________________

____

1. Packaged software [p. 1.13]

Packaged software is ______________________________

____

2. Custom software [p. 1.13]

Custom software is ______________________________

____

3. Shareware [p. 1.13]

   Shareware is ______________________________

   ____

4. Freeware and public-domain software [p. 1.13]

   - Freeware is ______________________________

     ____

   - Public-domain software is ______________________________

     ____

C. Software development [p. 1.13]

   Computer programmers write ______________________________

   A systems analyst manages ______________________________

VI. Networks and the Internet [p. 1.14]

A network is ______________________________

____

The Internet is ______________________________

____

People use the Internet to ______________________________

____

VII. Categories of computers [p. 1.18]

Computer categories are based on size, speed, processing capabilities, and price.

The four major categories of computers are:

- ______________
- ______________
- ______________
- ______________

VIII. Personal computers [p. 1.19]

A personal computer (PC) is ______________________________

____

A. Desktop computers [p. 1.20]

   A desktop computer is ______________________________

   ____

   A tower model has ______________________________

   ____

   1. Network computers [p. 1.22]

      Network computers are designed to ______________________________

      ____

B. Portable computers [p. 1.22]
A portable computer is ____________________

____

1. Laptop computers [p. 1.23]
A laptop computer is ____________________

____

2. Handheld computers [p. 1.23]
A handheld computer is ____________________

____

IX. Minicomputers [p. 1.24]
A minicomputer is ____________________

____

X. Mainframe computers [p. 1.24]
A mainframe is ____________________

____

XI. Supercomputers [p. 1.24]
A supercomputer is ____________________

____

XII. Examples of computer usage [p. 1.25]
Numerous users rely on different types of computers for a variety of applications.

A. Home user [p. 1.26]

____

____

B. Small business user [p. 1.28]

____

____

C. Mobile user [p. 1.30]

____

____

D. Large business user [p. 1.32]

____

____

E. Power user [p. 1.34]

____

____

Self Test

Matching

1. ____ input device
2. ____ output device
3. ____ system unit
4. ____ storage device
5. ____ communications device
6. ____ packaged software
7. ____ custom software
8. ____ shareware
9. ____ freeware
10. ____ public-domain software

a. software designed to meet the needs of a variety of users

b. used to enter data and commands into the memory of a computer

c. writes the instructions necessary to process data into information

d. programs developed at a user's request to perform specific functions

e. copyrighted software provided at no cost by an individual or company

f. houses the computer electronic circuitry, including the CPU and memory

g. enables computer users to exchange data, instructions, and information

h. collection of computers connected together via telephone lines, modems, or other means

i. software donated for general use with no copyright restrictions

j. records and retrieves data, instructions, and information to and from a medium

k. conveys information generated by a computer to a user

l. software distributed free for a trial period, after which a payment is sent to the developer

True/False

____ 1. As technology advances and computers extend into every facet of daily living, it is essential to gain some level of computer literacy.

____ 2. Without software, hardware is useless; hardware needs the instructions provided by software to process data into information.

____ 3. A mouse contains keys that allow you to type letters of the alphabet, numbers, spaces, punctuation marks, and other symbols.

____ 4. A peripheral device is any internal device inside the system unit.

____ 5. Storage differs from memory in that it holds items only temporarily while they are being processed, whereas memory can hold items permanently.

____ 6. When two or more computers are connected together via communications media and devices, they comprise a network.

____ 7. Before a computer can perform, or execute, a program, the instructions in the program must be placed, or loaded, into the memory of the computer.

____ 8. Hardware is the key to productive use of computers.

____ 9. Most users connect to the Internet in one of two ways: through an Internet service provider or through an online service.

____ 10. Small businesses seldom have a local area network to connect the computers in the company.

Multiple Choice

____ 1. How does information differ from data?
   a. information is a collection of unorganized facts
   b. information can include words, numbers, images, and sounds
   c. information is organized, has meaning, and is useful
   d. information is processed to produce data

____ 2. What are examples of input devices?
   a. the keyboard and the mouse
   b. the central processing unit (CPU) and memory
   c. the printer and the monitor
   d. all of the above

____ 3. What component is *not* considered a peripheral device?
   a. the keyboard
   b. the CPU
   c. a microphone
   d. a monitor

____ 4. Why is a computer so powerful?
   a. because of its capability to perform the information processing cycle operations with amazing speed, reliability, and accuracy
   b. because of its capacity to store huge amounts of data
   c. because of its ability to communicate with other computers
   d. all of the above

____ 5. What is application software?
   a. programs that coordinate all activities of hardware devices
   b. programs that serve as an interface between a user and the computer's hardware
   c. programs designed to perform specific tasks for users
   d. programs that control the operations of a computer and its devices

____ 6. Who writes the instructions necessary to direct a computer to process data into information?
   a. systems analysts
   b. mobile users
   c. programmers
   d. power users

____ 7. Why do people use the Internet?
   a. to send messages to other connected users
   b. to access a wealth of information
   c. to shop for goods and services
   d. all of the above

____ 8. What are workstations?
   a. large, expensive, very powerful computers that can handle hundreds or thousands of connected users simultaneously
   b. personal computers designed specifically to connect to a network, especially the Internet
   c. expensive, powerful desktop computers designed for work that requires intense calculations and graphics capabilities
   d. a popular type of handheld computers that often supports personal information management applications

____ 9. What is the most powerful category of computers and, accordingly, the most expensive?
   a. personal computers
   b. minicomputers
   c. mainframe computers
   d. supercomputers

____ 10. A local law practice, accounting firm, travel agency, and florist are examples of what type of computer user?
   a. mobile user
   b. small business user
   c. power user
   d. large business user

Fill in the Blanks

1. A(n) ____________________ is a person that communicates with a computer or employs the information it generates.
2. A(n) ____________________ is the physical material on which data, instructions, and information are stored.
3. A graphical user interface uses small visual images called ____________________ that represent programs, instructions, or some other object.
4. A(n) ____________________ is a collection of computers and devices connected together via communications media.

5. The world's largest network is the ____________________, a worldwide collection of networks that links together millions of computers.
6. A(n) ____________________ computer is not connected to a network and has the capability of performing the information processing cycle operations by itself.
7. A(n) ____________________ is a computer that manages the resources on a network.
8. Users often access a minicomputer via a(n) ____________________, which is a device with a monitor and a keyboard.
9. Many mobile users have a(n) ____________________, which is a platform where they place their laptops when in the main office.
10. A(n) ____________________ is a freestanding computer, usually with a touch screen that serves as an input device.

Complete the Table

CATEGORIES OF COMPUTERS

	Physical Size	*Number of instructions executed per second*	*Number of simultaneously connected users*
Personal Computer	Hand or desk size	____________	____________
Minicomputer	____________	Thousands to millions	____________
Mainframe	____________	____________	Hundreds to thousands
Supercomputer	Full room	____________	____________

Things to Think About

1. Do the four operations in the information processing cycle (input, process, output, storage) always have to be performed in order? Why or why not?
2. Why is each component of a computer system (input devices, system unit, output devices, secondary storage devices) important?
3. Why is software the key to productive use of computers?
4. Why do mobile users often have laptops equipped with a modem?

Puzzle

All of the words described below appear in the puzzle. Words may be either forward or backward, across, up and down, or diagonal. Circle each word as you find it.

Introduction to Using Computers

```
                  P E
                  D U
                  A S
      S T H       T E   J E K
    H A R D W A R E V R E S
  G S R E T U P M O C I N I M
  U T B T I N U M E T S Y S E
  I E M U L T I M E D I A G M
  N N C P U E R A W E E R F O
  P R F M A I N F R A M E J R
  U E W O R K S T A T I O N Y
  T T K C R E G A R O T S T A
    N S R E M M A R G O R P
    I O E S H A R E W A R E
      I P S O F T W A R E
      K U T E R M I N A L
        S T U P T U O A
        W K R O W T E N
            N O C I
```

interprets and carries out instructions

allows interaction using visual images

worldwide collection of networks

PC designed to connect to a network

computer that can perform all information processing activities

often supports PIM applications

process data into information

collection of unorganized facts

software provided at no cost to a user

electronic and mechanical equipment

small image that represents a program

organized, meaningful, useful data

data entered into a computer

freestanding computer, usually with a touch screen

can handle thousands of connected users

temporarily holds data and instructions

more powerful than a workstation

combines text, graphics, sound, video, and other elements

collection of connected computers

result of processing data

people who write computer instructions

manages network resources

software distributed free for a trial period

instructions to process data into information

where data is held for future use

fastest, most powerful computer

box-like case housing computer circuitry

device with a monitor and a keyboard

communicates with a computer or uses the information it generates

expensive and powerful desktop computer

Self Test Answers

Matching

1. *b* [p. 1.5]
2. *k* [p. 1.6]
3. *f* [p. 1.6]
4. *j* [p. 1.7]
5. *g* [p. 1.8]
6. *a* [p. 1.13]
7. *d* [p. 1.13]
8. *l* [p. 1.13]
9. *e* [p. 1.13]
0. *i* [p. 1.13]

True/False

1. *T* [p. 1.3]
2. *T* [p. 1.4]
3. *F* [p. 1.6]
4. *F* [p. 1.7]
5. *F* [p. 1.7]
6. *T* [p. 1.9]
7. *T* [p. 1.9]
8. *F* [p. 1.10]
9. *T* [p. 1.17]
0. *F* [p. 1.28]

Multiple Choice

1. *c* [p. 1.4]
2. *a* [p. 1.5]
3. *b* [p. 1.7]
4. *d* [p. 1.8]
5. *c* [p. 1.12]
6. *c* [p. 1.13]
7. *d* [p. 1.16]
8. *c* [p. 1.21]
9. *d* [p. 1.24]
0. *b* [p. 1.28]

Fill in the Blanks

1. *user* [p. 1.4]
2. *storage medium* [p. 1.7]
3. *icons* [p. 1.11]
4. *network* [p. 1.14]
5. *Internet* [p. 1.16]
6. *stand-alone* [p. 1.21]
7. *server* [p. 1.22]
8. *terminal* [p. 1.24]
9. *docking station* [p. 1.31]
0. *kiosk* [p. 1.33]

Complete the Table

CATEGORIES OF COMPUTERS

	Physical Size	*Number of instructions executed per second*	*Number of simultaneously connected users*
Personal Computer	Hand or desk size	*Up to 400 million*	*1 stand-alone or many networked*
Minicomputer	*Small cabinet*	Thousands to millions	*Two to 4,000*
Mainframe	*Partial to full room*	*Millions*	Hundreds to thousands
Supercomputer	Full room	*Millions to billions*	*Hundreds to thousands*

Things to Think About

Answers will vary.

Puzzle Answer

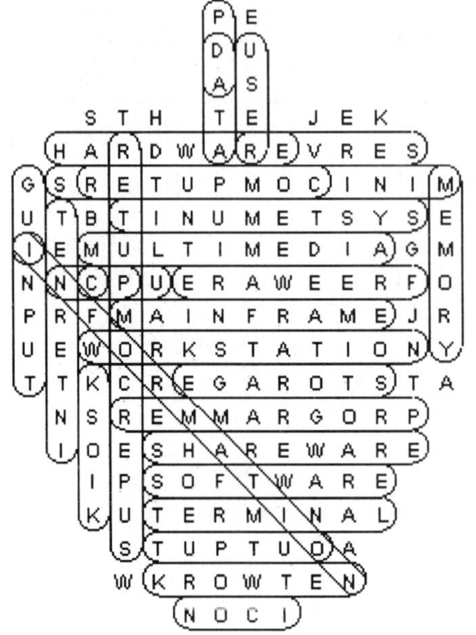

DISCOVERING COMPUTERS 2000

STUDY GUIDE

CHAPTER 2

Application Software and the World Wide Web

Chapter Overview

This chapter introduces computer software, the series of instructions that tells computer hardware how to perform tasks. You learn about application software and become acquainted with the role of the operating system, the role of the user interface, and the process of starting a software application. Various types of productivity software, graphics and multimedia software, software for personal and educational use, and software for communications are presented. You find out how to use a Web browser to connect to the World Wide Web, navigate Web pages, enter a URL, and search for information. Finally, you discover the learning aids and support tools available to help use an application software package or the Web more efficiently. Understanding the concepts presented in this chapter will help you advance toward your personal and professional goals.

Chapter Objectives

After completing this chapter, you should be able to:

- Define application software
- Explain how to start a software application
- Explain the key features of widely used software applications
- Provide examples illustrating the importance of the World Wide Web
- Describe how to use a Web browser
- Explain how to search for information on the Web
- Describe the learning aids available with many software applications

Chapter Outline

I. Application software [p. 2.2]

Application software, also called a software application or an application, consists of ____

A. The role of the operating system [p. 2.2]

The operating system contains ______________________________

____

The operating system must be loaded from the hard disk into the computer's memory before any application software can be run.

B. The role of the user interface [p. 2.3]

A user interface controls ______________________________

____

A graphical user interface (GUI) combines ______________________________

____

Windows (Microsoft Windows) is ______________________________

C. Starting a software application [p. 2.4]

The desktop is an onscreen work area that uses common graphical elements to make the computer easier to use. Graphical elements include:

- Icons – ______________________________
- Buttons – ______________________________
- Menus – ______________________________
- Windows – ______________________________
- Dialog boxes – ______________________________

You can start an application by clicking its name on a menu or submenu.

II. Productivity software [p. 2.7]

Productivity software is ______________________________

____

A. Word processing software [p. 2.8]

Word processing software is used to ______________________________

____

1. Developing a document [p. 2.8]
   - Creating involves ______________________________

     ____
   - Editing is ______________________________

     ____
   - Formatting involves ______________________________

     ____

     A font is ______________________________

     Font size specifies ______________________________

     Font style adds ______________________________
   - Saving is ______________________________

     ____

A file is ____

A file name is ____

- Printing is ____

  ____

2. Basic word processing features [p. 2.10]
   - Borders – ______________________________________
   - Clip art – ______________________________________
   - Margins – ______________________________________
   - Wordwrap – _____________________________________
   - Scrolling – _____________________________________
   - Find or search – _________________________________
   - Replace – ______________________________________
   - Spelling checker – _______________________________
   - Headers and footers – ____________________________

B. Spreadsheet software [p. 2.12]

Spreadsheet software allows ______________________________________

____

1. Spreadsheet organization [p. 2.12]

   On a worksheet, data is organized vertically in columns and horizontally in rows. A letter identifies each column, and a number identifies each row.

   A cell is ____

   Cells are identified by the column and row in which they are located (e.g., the cell at column B and row 10 is referred to as cell _______).

   Cells may contain three types of data:
   - _______________ (text)
   - _______________ (numbers)
   - _______________ (calculations performed on data)

2. Calculations [p. 2.13]

   A formula performs ______________________________________

   A function is ____

3. Macros [p. 2.13]

   A macro is ____

   ____

4. Recalculation [p. 2.14]

   A powerful spreadsheet feature is that when data changes, the rest of the data in a worksheet is recalculated automatically.

What-if analysis is ______________________________

____

5. Charting [p. 2.14]

Charting displays data relationships in a graphical, rather than numerical, form. Popular chart types include:

- ______________ • ______________ • ______________

C. Database software [p. 2.15]

A database is ______________________________

____

Database software allows ______________________________

____

Most PC databases consist of a collection of tables.

- A record is ______________________________
- A field is ______________________________

1. Database organization [p. 2.16]

The table structure is the number of fields, the field names, the field lengths, and the data types in the database table.

Field names should be short yet descriptive.

Field length is ______________________________

Data type specifies ______________________________

Common data types:

- ______________ • ______________ • ______________
- ______________ • ______________ • ______________

2. Entering data [p. 2.17]

Validation is ______________________________

____

3. Manipulating data [p. 2.17]

Once records are entered, database software can be used to manipulate the data to generate information.

- Sort ______________________________

  ____

- A query ______________________________

  ____

D. Presentation graphics software [p. 2.18]

Presentation graphics software allows ______________________________

____

A clip gallery includes ______________________________

____

E. Personal information managers [p. 2.21]

A personal information manager (PIM) is ______________________________

____

Most PIMs include:

- __________ • __________ • __________

F. Software suite [p. 2.21]

A software suite is ______________________________

____

G. Project management software [p. 2.22]

Project management software allows ______________________________

____

H. Accounting software [p. 2.22]

Accounting software helps ______________________________

____

III. Graphics and multimedia software [p. 2.23]

A. Computer-aided design [p. 2.24]

Computer-aided design (CAD) software is ______________________________

____

B. Desktop publishing software (professional) [p. 2.24]

Desktop publishing (DTP) software allows ______________________________

____

DTP software is designed to support page layout, which is ______________

____

C. Paint/Image editing software (professional) [p. 2.25]

Paint software (illustration software) allows ______________________________

____

Image editing software provides ______________________________

____

D. Video and audio editing software [p. 2.26]

Video consists of ______________________________

Video editing software can be used to ______________________________

____

Audio is ____

Audio editing software can be used to ______________________________

____

E. Multimedia authoring software [p. 2.26]

Multimedia authoring software is ______________________________

____

F. Web page authoring software [p. 2.27]

Web page authoring software is ______________________________

____

IV. Software for home, personal, and educational use [p. 2.27]

A. Integrated software [p. 2.28]

Integrated software is ______________________________

____

B. Personal finance software [p. 2.28]

Personal finance software is ______________________________

____

C. Legal software [p. 2.29]

Legal software assists in ______________________________

____

D. Tax preparation software [p. 2.29]

Tax preparation software guides ______________________________

____

E. Desktop publishing (personal) [p. 2.30]

Personal DTP software can be used to ______________________________

____

F. Paint/Image editing software (personal) [p. 2.30]

Personal paint/image editing software provides an easy-to-use interface, usually with more simplified capabilities than its professional counterpart. Photo-editing software, a type of image editing software, allows ____________

____

G. Clip art/Image gallery [p. 2.31]

A clip art/image gallery is ______________________________

H. Home design/landscaping software [p. 2.31]

Home design/landscaping software is used to ______________________________

____

I. Educational/reference/personal computer entertainment software [p. 2.32]

- Educational software is ______
- Reference software provides ______
- Personal computer entertainment software includes ______

V. Software for communications [p. 2.32]

A. Groupware [p. 2.32]

Groupware identifies ______

B. Electronic mail software [p. 2.33]

E-mail (electronic mail) is ______

Electronic mail software is used to ______

An e-mail address is ______

Components of a sample e-mail address:

______ ➩ ☜ ______

SallyJohnson @ scsite.com

C. Web browsers [p. 2.34]

A Web browser, or browser, allows ______

VI. Browsing the World Wide Web [p. 2.35]

The World Wide Web (WWW), or Web, consists of ______

Web pages can contain ______

Web sites are ______

A. Connecting to the Web and starting a browser [p. 2.36]

You can connect to the Internet through an Internet service provider, an online service, or a network connected to an Internet service provider.

An Internet service provider (ISP) is ______

An online service provides ______

B. Navigating Web pages using links [p. 2.37]

A hyperlink, or link, is ______________________________

To activate a link, you click it.

Surfing the Web is ______________________________

C. Using the browser toolbars [p. 2.39]

Browser toolbar buttons can be used to navigate and work with Web sites.

D. Entering a URL [p. 2.39]

A Uniform Resource Locator (URL) is ______________________________

____

Most Web page URLs begin with http://, which stands for ______________

____

A Web server is ______________________________

E. Searching for information on the Web [p. 2.40]

A search engine is ______________________________

____

VII. Learning aids and support tools [p. 2.42]

Learning aids provided by many applications and Web sites:

- Online help is ______________________________
- FAQs are ______________________________
- Tutorials are ______________________________
- A wizard is ______________________________

Self Test

Matching

1. ____ computer-aided design (CAD) software
2. ____ desktop publishing (DTP) software
3. ____ paint software
4. ____ multimedia authoring software
5. ____ personal finance software
6. ____ legal software
7. ____ tax preparation software
8. ____ home design/landscaping software
9. ____ educational software
10. ____ electronic mail software

a. used to prepare judicial documents and provide statutory advice

b. used to create electronic interactive presentations that include a variety of elements

c. used to create, send, receive, forward, store, print, and delete e-mail messages

d. used in creating engineering, architectural, and scientific designs

e. used to pay bills, balance a checkbook, track income and expenses, and monitor investments

f. used to guide individuals or small businesses through the process of filing federal taxes

g. used to draw pictures, shapes, and other graphical images with various screen tools

h. used to edit digital photographs by removing red-eye or adding special effects

i. used to create Web pages, in addition to organizing and maintaining Web sites

j. used to design and produce sophisticated documents containing text and graphics

k. used to assist with the design or remodeling of a house, deck, or yard

l. used to teach a particular skill, from a foreign language to how to cook

True/False

____ 1. A graphical user interface (GUI) combines animation, sound, and other audio clues to make software easier to use.

____ 2. Shortcut menus display a list of commands commonly used to complete a task related to the current activity or selected item.

____ 3. Formatting is important because the overall look of a document can significantly affect its ability to communicate effectively.

____ 4. A header is text that appears at the bottom of each page.

____ 5. Only a small fraction of the columns and rows in a spreadsheet displays on the computer screen at one time.

____ 6. In a database, a field contains information about a given person, product, or event, while a record contains a specific piece of information within a field.

____ 7. Presentation graphics software provides an array of predefined presentation formats that define complementary colors and other items on the slides.

____ 8. Precisely defining a PIM is easy because personal information managers offer only a single capability.

____ 9. The applications within an integrated software package typically have all the capabilities of stand-alone productivity applications.

____ 10. Web page links allow you to obtain information in a nonlinear way through associations between topics, instead of moving sequentially through topics.

Multiple Choice

____ 1. What must be loaded, or copied, into memory from the computer's hard disk each time you start your computer?
   a. the operating system
   b. a software application
   c. the software package
   d. a utility program

____ 2. What is a title bar?
   a. a small image that displays on the screen to represent a program
   b. an onscreen work area that uses common graphical elements
   c. a horizontal space at the top of a window that displays the window's name
   d. an instruction that causes a computer program to perform a specific action

____ 3. When developing a document, what happens during the formatting activity?
   a. text, numbers, or graphical images are inserted using an input device
   b. changes are made to the document's existing content
   c. the appearance of the document is changed
   d. all of the above

____ 4. How many rows and columns does a spreadsheet typically have?
   a. 256 rows and 256 columns
   b. 65,536 rows and 65,536 columns
   c. 256 rows and 65,536 columns
   d. 65,536 rows and 256 columns

____ 5. What common data type includes freeform text of any kind or length?
   a. numeric
   b. memo
   c. hyperlink
   d. currency

____ 6. In a personal information manager, for what purpose is a notepad used?
a. to record ideas, reminders, and other important information
b. to schedule activities for a particular day and time
c. to enter and maintain names, addresses, and telephone numbers
d. to design and produce sophisticated documents

____ 7. What type of software might a general contractor use to manage a home-remodeling schedule or a publisher use to coordinate the process of producing a textbook?
a. home design/landscaping software
b. project management software
c. desktop publishing software
d. presentation graphics software

____ 8. What type of software can be used to modify sound clips and usually includes filters designed to enhance sound quality?
a. audio editing software
b. video editing software
c. image editing software
d. photo-editing software

____ 9. Which of the following is *not* an informal rule for using e-mail?
a. use all capital letters for confidential messages
b. keep messages brief using proper grammar and spelling
c. use emoticons to express emotion
d. be careful when using sarcasm and humor

____ 10. What does word processing software use to help you create memorandums, meeting agendas, fax cover sheets, and letters?
a. online help
b. FAQs
c. tutorials
d. wizards

Fill in the Blanks

1. A specific software product, such as Microsoft Word, often is called a(n) ____________________.
2. In a graphical user interface, ____________________ are instructions that cause a computer program to perform a specific action.
3. Cutting involves removing a portion of a document and electronically storing it in a temporary storage location called the ____________________.
4. A(n) ____________________ is a predefined formula that performs common calculations or generates a value in a spreadsheet.
5. The number of fields, field names, field lengths, and data types in a database table collectively are referred to as the table ____________________.

6. A(n) ____________________ includes clip art images, pictures, video clips, and audio clips that can be used in a presentation.
7. A(n) ____________________ is a standard set of colors included in DTP packages that is used to ensure that colors will print exactly as specified.
8. When you receive an e-mail message, it is placed in your ____________________, which is a storage location usually residing on the computer that connects you to the local area network or the Internet.
9. The process of receiving information, such as a Web page, onto your computer from a server on the Internet is called ____________________.
10. To find Web pages on specific topics, you enter a word or phrase, called ____________________, in a search engine text box, and the search engine then displays a list of all Web pages that contain the word or phrase.

Complete the Table

POPULAR SOFTWARE PACKAGES FOR HOME/PERSONAL/EDUCATIONAL USE

Software Application	Popular Packages
____________________	• Microsoft Works
____________________	• Intuit Quicken
____________________	• WillMaker
____________________	• Kiplinger TaxCut
____________________	• Corel Gallery
____________________	• Autodesk Planix Complete Home Suite
____________________	• Microsoft Encarta

Things to Think About

1. What word processing features would be most useful to an author composing a short story? To a publicist creating a newsletter? To a student writing a term paper? Why?
2. Why is a spreadsheet's capability to perform what-if analysis important to business executives?
3. What types of software would be particularly useful to business travelers? Why?
4. Why are each of the informal rules for using e-mail (see Figure 2-44 on page 2.34) important?

Puzzle

Use the given clues to complete the crossword puzzle.

Application Software and the WWW

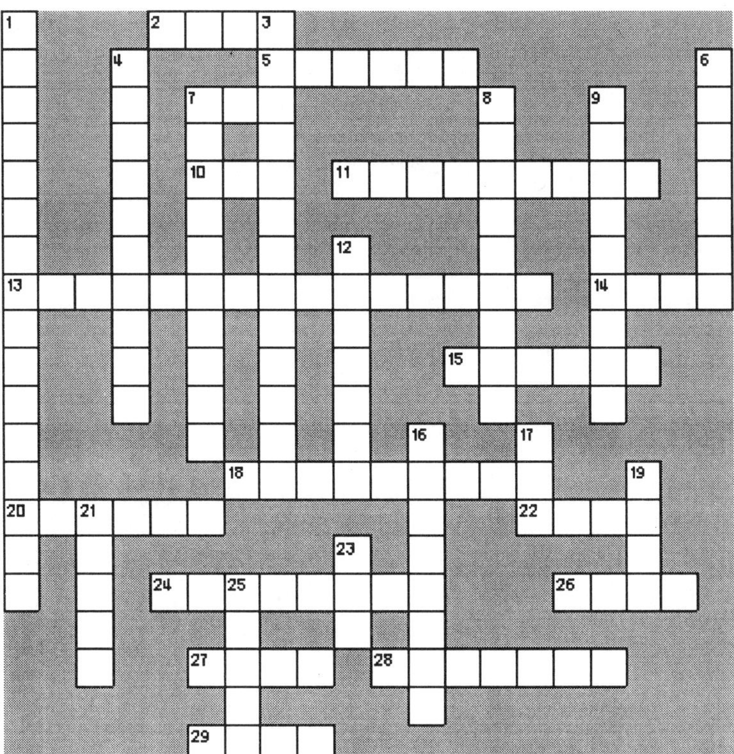

Across

2. Contains commands that can be selected
5. Copying a document to a storage medium
7. Chart type that shows relationship of parts to the whole
10. Combines text, graphics, and other visual clues
11. Information at the bottom of an e-mail message
13. Specific software product
14. Stands for hypertext transfer protocol
15. Decorative line around document edges
18. Computer that delivers requested Web pages
20. Bring clip art into a word processing document
22. Chart type effective for showing trends
24. Starting page for a Web site
26. Named collection of data, instructions, or information
27. Small image representing a program or document
28. Today's most widely used PC operating system
29. Name assigned to a specific character design

Down

1. Help information related to the current task
3. Controls how information is entered and presented
4. Comparing data to predefined rules or values
6. Onscreen work area
7. Arranging DTP text and graphics
8. Provides information or requests a response
9. Collection of spreadsheet rows and columns
12. Portion of page outside main body of text
16. Restrictions that queried data must meet
17. Unique Web page address
19. Intersection of a row and column
21. About 1/72 of an inch in height
23. Chart type that shows data relationships
25. Recorded sequence of keystrokes and instructions

Self Test Answers

Matching

1. *d* [p. 2.24]
2. *j* [p. 2.24]
3. *g* [p. 2.25]
4. *b* [p. 2.26]
5. *e* [p. 2.28]
6. *a* [p. 2.29]
7. *f* [p. 2.29]
8. *k* [p. 2.31]
9. *l* [p. 2.32]
0. *c* [p. 2.33]

True/False

1. *F* [p. 2.3]
2. *T* [p. 2.6]
3. *T* [p. 2.9]
4. *F* [p. 2.11]
5. *T* [p. 2.12]
6. *F* [p. 2.15]
7. *T* [p. 2.18]
8. *F* [p. 2.21]
9. *F* [p. 2.28]
0. *T* [p. 2.37]

Multiple Choice

1. *a* [p. 2.3]
2. *c* [p. 2.4]
3. *c* [p. 2.9]
4. *d* [p. 2.12]
5. *b* [p. 2.16]
6. *a* [p. 2.21]
7. *b* [p. 2.22]
8. *a* [p. 2.26]
9. *a* [p. 2.34]
0. *d* [p. 2.43]

Fill in the Blanks

1. *software package* [p. 2.2]
2. *commands* [p. 2.4]
3. *Clipboard* [p. 2.8]
4. *function* [p. 2.13]
5. *structure* [p. 2.16]
6. *clip gallery* [p. 2.19]
7. *color library* [p. 2.25]
8. *mailbox* [p. 2.33]
9. *downloading* [p. 2.37]
0. *search text* or *keywords* [p. 2.40]

Complete the Table

POPULAR SOFTWARE PACKAGES FOR HOME/PERSONAL/EDUCATIONAL USE

Software Application	Popular Packages
Integrated Software	• Microsoft Works
Personal Finance	• Intuit Quicken
Legal	• WillMaker
Tax Preparation	• Kiplinger TaxCut
Clip Art/Image Gallery	• Corel Gallery
Home Design/Landscaping	• Autodesk Planix Complete Home Suite
Reference	• Microsoft Encarta

Things to Think About

Answers will vary.

Puzzle Answer

Application Software and the WWW

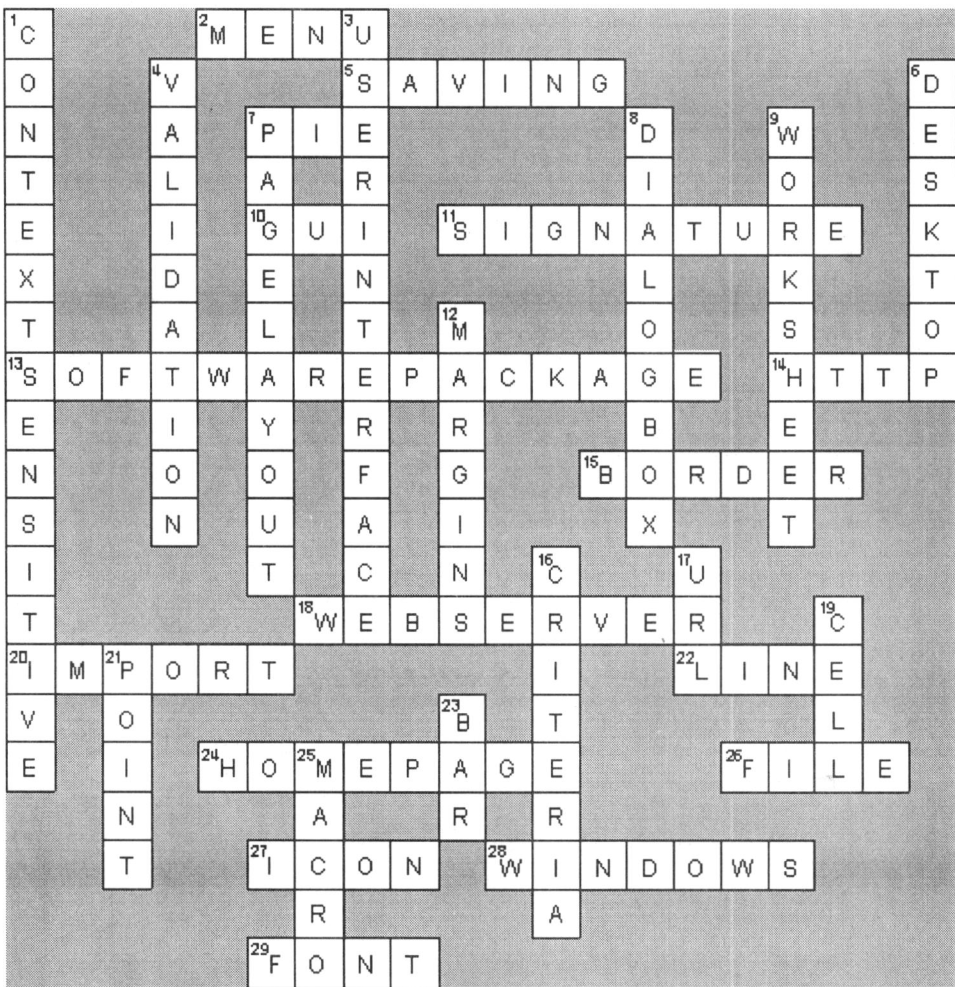

DISCOVERING COMPUTERS 2000

STUDY GUIDE

CHAPTER 3

The Components in the System Unit

Chapter Overview

This chapter examines the system unit. The motherboard is introduced, and the CPU and its components – the control unit and the arithmetic/logic unit – are described. You learn about pipelining, popular microprocessors, registers, the system clock, processor installation and upgrades, heat sinks and heat pipes, coprocessors, and parallel processing. You discover how data is represented. Different types of memory, including RAM, RAM cache, ROM, and CMOS, and the importance of memory access time are explored. You find out how expansion slots and expansion cards, ports, buses, and bays are used to connect devices to the motherboard. The power supply and the laptop computer system unit are explained. Finally, configurations are suggested for various users.

Chapter Objectives

After completing this chapter, you should be able to:

- Identify the components in the system unit and explain their functions
- Explain how the CPU uses the four steps of a machine cycle to process data
- Compare and contrast various microprocessors on the market today
- Define a bit and describe how a series of bits is used to represent data
- Differentiate between the various types of memory
- Describe the types of expansion slots and expansion cards in the system unit
- Explain the difference between a serial and a parallel port
- Describe how buses contribute to a computer's processing speed

Chapter Outline

I. The system unit [p. 3.2]

The system unit is ____

____

A. The motherboard [p. 3.4]

Many of the electronic components in the system unit reside on a circuit board called the ______________________________

1. Chips [p. 3.4]

A chip is ______________________________

____

An integrated circuit is ______________________________

____

II. CPU and microprocessor [p. 3.5]

The central processing unit (CPU or processor) ______________________________

____

On a PC, the CPU is contained on a single chip called a microprocessor. A microprocessor usually contains the control unit, the arithmetic/logic unit, registers, and the system clock.

A. The control unit [p. 3.6]

The control unit ______________________________

____

The control unit repeats a set of four basic operations called the machine cycle or instruction cycle:

- Fetching ______________________________
- Decoding ______________________________
- Executing ______________________________
- Storing ______________________________

Some computer professionals measure a computer's speed in MIPS (**mi**llions of **i**nstructions processed **p**er **s**econd).

B. The arithmetic/logic unit [p. 3.7]

The arithmetic/logic unit (ALU) ______________________________

____

The ALU performs three operations:

- Arithmetic operations ______________________________
- Comparison operations ______________________________
- Logical operations ______________________________

C. Pipelining [p. 3.7]

Some computers speed processing with pipelining, in which the CPU ________

____

D. Registers [p. 3.8]

Registers are ______________________________

E. The system clock [p. 3.8]

The system clock ______________________________

____

Clock speed (the speed at which a processor executes instructions) is measured in ______________________________

F. Microprocessor comparison [p. 3.9]

PCs use Intel (such as Pentium® and Celeron™) and Intel-compatible microprocessors. Apple computers use Motorola microprocessors. When buying a computer, clock speed is an important consideration.

G. Processor installation and upgrades [p. 3.10]

A zero-insertion force (ZIF) socket has ______________________________

____

H. Heat sinks and heat pipes [p. 3.10]

A heat sink is ______________________________

____

A heat pipe is a smaller device used to cool laptop computers.

I. Coprocessors [p. 3.11]

A coprocessor is ______________________________

____

J. Parallel processing [p 3.11]

Parallel processing speeds processing time by using ______________________________

____

III. Data representation [p. 3.11]

Most computers are digital, meaning ______________________________

____

Computers use the binary number system, which has only two digits, to represent the electronic states of off (0) and on (1).

A bit is ______________________________

A byte is ______________________________

Popular patterns, or coding schemes, used to represent data:

- ______________
- ______________
- ______________

IV. Memory [p. 3.14]

In the system unit, a computer's memory stores three basic items:

(1) ______________________________

(2) ______________________________

(3) ______________________________

An address is a unique number identifying the location of a byte in memory.

Memory can be volatile or nonvolatile.

The contents of volatile memory are ______________________________

The contents of nonvolatile memory are ______________________________

A. RAM [p. 3.15]

RAM (random access memory) ______________________________

____

Basic types of RAM:

- Dynamic RAM (DRAM) ______________________________

  Synchronous DRAM (SDRAM) is ______________________________
- Static RAM (SRAM) is ______________________________

1. RAM chips [p. 3.16]

   RAM chips usually are packaged ______________________________

   ____

2. Configuring RAM [p. 3.16]

   The necessary amount of RAM varies according to ______________________________

   ____

B. Cache [p. 3.17]

Memory cache speeds processing by ______________________________

- Level 1 (L1) cache is ______________________________
- Level 2 (L2) cache consists of ______________________________

1. Configuring cache [p. 3.18]

   To realize the largest increase in performance, a system should have from

   ____

C. ROM [p. 3.18]

ROM (read-only memory) ______________________________

____

A programmable read-only memory (PROM) chip is a type of ROM chip on which you can permanently place items.

1. Flash memory [p. 3.18]

   Flash memory is ______________________________

   ____

D. CMOS [p 3.19]

   CMOS (complementary metal-oxide semiconductor memory) is __________

   ____

E. Memory access times [p. 3.19]

   Access time is ______________________________

   For memory, access times are measured in ______________________________

V. Expansion slots and expansion cards [p. 3.20]

An expansion slot is a socket where a circuit board, or expansion card, can be inserted into the motherboard to add new devices, or capabilities, to the computer.

Types of expansion cards:

- __________ • __________ • __________

Plug and Play refers to ______________________________

A. PC Cards [p. 3.21]

   A PC Card is ______________________________

   ____

VI. Ports [p. 3.21]

A port is ______________________________

Ports have different types of connectors, which are used to join a cable to a device.

- Male connectors have ______________________________
- Female connectors have ______________________________

A. Serial ports [p. 3.23]

   A serial port transmits______________________________

   Serial ports are used to connect ______________________________

B. Parallel ports [p. 3.23]

   A parallel port transfers ______________________________

   Parallel ports are used to connect ______________________________

C. Special-purpose ports [p. 3.24]

   1. MIDI (musical instrument digital interface) port [p. 3.24]

      A MIDI port ______________________________

   2. SCSI (small computer system interface) port [p. 3.24]

      A SCSI port______________________________

3. Universal serial bus (USB) port [p. 3.24]

   A USB port ______________________________

4. 1394 port [p. 3.24]

   A 1394 port ______________________________

5. IrDA (Infrared Data Association) port [p. 3.24]

   An IrDA port ______________________________

VII. Buses [p. 3.24]

A bus is an electrical channel that ______________________________

____

The bus width, or size of the bus, determines ______________________________

Word size is ______________________________

A system bus ______________________________

An expansion bus ______________________________

A. Expansion bus [p. 3.26]

The types of expansion buses on the motherboard determine the types of expansion cards you can add.

Types of expansion buses:

- ________ • ________ • ________
- ________ • ________ • ________

VIII. Bays [p. 3.27]

A bay is ______________________________

Drive bays ______________________________

- An external drive bay ______________________________
- An internal drive bay ______________________________

IX. Power supply [p. 3.28]

The power supply is the component in the system unit that ______________________________

____

X. Laptop computers [p. 3.28]

Like desktop computers, laptop computers have a system unit that contains electronic components used to process data. In addition, a laptop computer's system unit also houses devices such as ______________________________

A port replicator is ______________________________

Self Test

Matching

1. ____ MIDI port
2. ____ ISA bus
3. ____ SCSI port
4. ____ VESA bus
5. ____ AGP
6. ____ PCI bus
7. ____ USB port
8. ____ 1394 bus
9. ____ IrDA port
10. ____ PC Card bus

a. bus that speeds processing by storing frequently used instructions and data

b. expansion bus for a PC Card that adds capabilities to a laptop computer

c. port used by wireless devices to transmit signals to a computer

d. port that can connect up to 127 different devices with a single connector

e. the most common and slowest expansion bus; connects to a mouse and modem card

f. first standard local expansion bus, which was used primarily for video cards

g. port designed to absorb and ventilate heat produced by electrical components

h. special high-speed parallel port used to attach disk drives and printers

i. bus designed by Intel to improve the speed with which graphics and video are transmitted

j. bus that eliminates the need to install expansion cards into expansion slots

k. special type of serial port designed to connect the system unit to a musical instrument

l. current local bus standard, used with video cards and high-speed network cards

True/False

____ 1. On a desktop personal computer, the electronic components and most storage devices reside outside the system unit.

____ 2. The time it takes to fetch an instruction is called instruction time or I-time, while the time it takes to decode and execute an instruction is called execution time or E-time.

____ 3. A brand of Intel processor called the Xeon™ is designed for less expensive PCs.

____ 4. The American Standard Code for Information Interchange (ASCII) is used primarily on mainframe computers.

____ 5. When a computer is turned on, certain operating system files are loaded from a storage device and remain in RAM as long as the computer is running.

____ 6. A single inline memory module (SIMM) has RAM chips on both sides.

____ 7. A millisecond (ms), a measure of hard disk access time, is one millionth of a second.

____ 8. An internal modem is a communications device that enables computers to communicate via telephone lines.

____ 9. The ability to add and remove devices while a computer is running is called hot plugging or hot swapping.

____ 10. An AC adapter converts a standard wall outlet's DC power of 5 to 12 volts to the AC power ranging from 115 to 120 volts that is required for use with a computer.

Multiple Choice

____ 1. In a desktop computer, what normally is located *outside* the system unit?
   a. expansion cards
   b. the processor and memory module
   c. ports and connectors
   d. the keyboard and monitor

____ 2. In the machine cycle, what is the process of decoding?
   a. obtaining an instruction or data item from memory
   b. translating an instruction into command a computer understands
   c. carrying out the commands
   d. writing a result to memory

____ 3. What microprocessor, developed by Digital Equipment Corporation, is used primarily in workstations and high-end servers?
   a. the Celeron™ microprocessor
   b. the Motorola microprocessor
   c. the Pentium® microprocessor
   d. the Alpha microprocessor

____ 4. A group of eight bits, called a byte, provides enough different combinations of 0s and 1s to represent how many individual characters?
   a. 8
   b. 16
   c. 256
   d. 1024

____ 5. Which of the following is an example of volatile memory?
   a. RAM
   b. ROM
   c. CMOS
   d. all of the above

____ 6. In general, home users running Windows and using standard application software such as word processing should have at least how much RAM?
a. 32 MB
b. 64 MB
c. 128 MB
d. 256 MB

____ 7. When a processor needs an instruction or data, in what order does it search memory?
a. first RAM, then L1 cache, then L2 cache
b. first L1 cache, then RAM, then L2 cache
c. first L2 cache, then RAM, then L1 cache
d. first L1 cache, then L2 cache, then RAM

____ 8. What type of PC Cards are used to house devices such as hard disks?
a. Type I cards
b. Type II cards
c. Type III cards
d. Type IV cards

____ 9. Originally developed as an alternative to the slower speed serial ports, parallel ports often are used to connect what to the system unit?
a. a mouse
b. a keyboard
c. a modem
d. a printer

____ 10. Like the clock speed at which a processor executes, the clock speed for a bus is measured in what unit?
a. milliseconds (ms)
b. megahertz (MHz)
c. nanoseconds (ns)
d. kilobytes (KB)

Fill in the Blanks

1. An integrated circuit can contain millions of elements such as ________________, which act as electronic switches, or gates, that open or close the circuit for electronic signals.
2. Most of today's processors are ____________________, which means they can execute more than one instruction per clock cycle.
3. Users of multimedia applications should obtain an Intel processor equipped with ____________________, in which a set of instructions are built into the processor so it can manipulate and process multimedia data more efficiently.
4. In contrast to most computers, human speech is ____________________, meaning that it uses continuous signals to represent data and information.

5. Unlike ASCII and EBCDIC, ____________________ is a coding scheme capable of representing all of the world's current languages.
6. When discussing RAM, users normally are referring to ____________________, a type of memory that must be re-energized constantly or it loses its contents.
7. ROM chips that contain permanently written data, instructions, or information are called ____________________.
8. For memory, access times are measured in terms of a(n) ____________________, which is one billionth of a second.
9. A(n) ____________________ is a device that can be used to join two connectors that are either both female or both male.
10. A(n) ____________________, which can be a peripheral or a chip, creates sound from digital instructions.

Complete the Table

MEMORY AND STORAGE SIZES

Term	*Abbreviation*	*Approximate Memory Size*	*Approximate Number of Pages of Text*
____________	KB or K	1 thousand bytes	____________
Megabyte	____________	____________	50,000
____________	GB	____________	50,000,000
____________	____________	1 trillion bytes	50,000,000,000

Things to Think About

1. If you were to purchase a computer today, what type of microprocessor would it have? Why?
2. Why do people upgrade their processors instead of buying a new computer? What form of processor upgrade seems easiest? Why?
3. How do coding schemes make it possible for humans to interact with computers? Why do people usually not realize that coding scheme conversions are occurring?
4. How is the system unit for a laptop computer similar to, and different from, the system unit for a desktop computer? Why do you think a laptop computer usually is more expensive than a desktop computer with the same capabilities?

Puzzle

Write the word described by each clue in the puzzle below. Words can be written forward or backward, across, up and down, or diagonally. The initial letter of each word already appears in the puzzle.

								C	C		A
M											
					C			E			
			M		R						B
D											
			S				M				
A					B						
			C	Z			B				
						L					
						D					
F								B		C	
				L							P

because most computers are this type, the data they process must first be converted into a numeric value

smallest unit of data handled by a computer

a group of eight bits

most widely used coding system to represent data

coding system primarily used on mainframe computers

used to join a cable to a device

contains the control unit and the arithmetic/logic unit

can be thought of as the *brain* of the computer

machine cycle operation referring to the actual processing of the computer commands

contains the electronic circuitry necessary to perform arithmetic and logical operations on data

type of operations that consists of comparing one data item to another

name given to the integrated circuits, or chips, that are used for main memory

approximately one million bytes

today, most RAM memory is installed by using this

type of RAM chips that comprises main memory, with access speeds of 50 to 100 nanoseconds

instructions stored in ROM memory

a special microprocessor chip or circuit board designed to perform a specific task

any path along which bits can be transmitted

type of expansion bus that connects directly to the type of cards used for additional memory, storage, and communications

type of ports that can transfer eight bits (one byte) at a time

type of serial port designed to be connected to a musical device

an open area inside the system unit used to install additional equipment

small piece of semiconducting material on which one or more integrated circuits are etched

part of a machine language instruction that specifies the data or the location of the data that will be used

socket designed to facilitate the installation and removal of processor chips

one million instructions per second

Self Test Answers

Matching

1. *k* [p. 3.24]
2. *e* [p. 3.26]
3. *h* [p. 3.24]
4. *f* [p. 3.27]
5. *i* [p. 3.27]
6. *l* [p. 3.27]
7. *d* [p. 3.24]
8. *j* [p. 3.27]
9. *c* [p. 3.24]
0. *b* [p. 3.27]

True/False

1. *F* [p. 3.2]
2. *T* [p. 3.6]
3. *F* [p. 3.9]
4. *F* [p. 3.12]
5. *T* [p. 3.15]
6. *F* [p. 3.16]
7. *F* [p. 3.20]
8. *T* [p. 3.20]
9. *T* [p. 3.21]
0. *F* [p. 3.28]

Multiple Choice

1. *d* [p. 3.3]
2. *b* [p. 3.6]
3. *d* [p. 3.9]
4. *c* [p. 3.12]
5. *a* [p. 3.15]
6. *a* [p. 3.16]
7. *d* [p. 3.17]
8. *c* [p. 3.21]
9. *d* [p. 3.23]
0. *b* [p. 3.26]

Fill in the Blanks

1. *transistors* [p. 3.4]
2. *superscalar* [p. 3.8]
3. *MMX™ technology* [p. 3.10]
4. *analog* [p. 3.11]
5. *Unicode* [p. 3.12]
6. *dynamic RAM* or *DRAM* [p. 3.16]
7. *firmware* [p. 3.18]
8. *nanosecond (ns)* [p. 3.19]
9. *gender changer* [p. 3.22]
0. *synthesizer* [p. 3.24]

Complete the Table

MEMORY AND STORAGE SIZES

Term	*Abbreviation*	*Approximate Memory Size*	*Approximate Number of Pages of Text*
Kilobyte	KB or K	1 thousand bytes	*50*
Megabyte	*MB*	*1 million bytes*	50,000
Gigabyte	GB	*1 billion bytes*	50,000,000
Terabyte	*TB*	1 trillion bytes	50,000,000,000

Things to Think About

Answers will vary.

Puzzle Answer

R	O	T	C	E	N	N	O	**C**	**C**	T	**A**
M	E	G	A	B	Y	T	E	P	O	I	L
G	N	I	T	U	**C**	E	X	**E**	P	N	U
S	P	I	**M**	A	**R**	P	B	R	R	U	**B**
D	Y	N	A	M	I	C	U	A	O	L	U
M	M	I	**S**	I	D	I	**M**	N	C	O	S
A	S	C	I	I	**B**	I	T	D	E	R	A
P	I	H	**C**	**Z**	I	F	**B**	E	S	T	I
L	A	C	I	G	O	**L**	A	T	S	N	C
L	A	T	I	G	I	**D**	Y	Y	O	O	M
F	I	R	M	W	A	R	E	**B**	R	**C**	C
L	A	C	O	**L**	E	L	L	A	R	A	**P**

DISCOVERING COMPUTERS 2000

STUDY GUIDE

CHAPTER 4

Input

Chapter Overview

In this chapter, you learn what is input and what are input devices. The keyboard is presented and different keyboard types are described. You are introduced to various pointing devices, such as the mouse, trackball, touchpad, pointing stick, joystick, touch screen, and pen input. Scanners and reading devices, including optical scanners, optical readers, magnetic ink character recognition readers, and data collection devices are explained. You learn about digital cameras, audio input, speech recognition, video input, and videoconferencing. Finally, input devices for physically challenged users are explored.

Chapter Objectives

After completing this chapter, you should be able to:

- Describe the four types of input
- List the characteristics of a keyboard
- Identify various types of keyboards
- Identify various types of pointing devices
- Explain how a mouse works
- Describe different mouse types
- Explain how scanners and other reading devices work
- Identify the purpose of a digital camera
- Describe the various techniques used for audio and video input
- Identify alternative input devices for physically challenged users

Chapter Outline

I. What is input? [p. 4.2]

Input is ______________________________

____

Types of input:

- Data is ______________________________

  ____

- A program is ______________________________

  ____

- A command is ______________________________
  ____
- A user response is ______________________________
  ____

II. What are input devices? [p. 4.3]
An input device is ______________________________
____

III. The keyboard [p. 4.3]
A keyboard is ______________________________
Many computer keyboards include:
- A typing area that includes letters of the alphabet, numbers, spaces, punctuation marks, and other basic keys.
- A numeric keypad ______________________________
  ____
- Function keys ______________________________
  ____
- Arrow keys ______________________________
  ____
- Toggle keys ______________________________
  ____

A. Keyboard types [p. 4.6]
   - QWERTY keyboard ______________________________
     ____
   - Dvorak keyboard ______________________________
     ____
   - Enhanced keyboards ______________________________
     ____
   - Wireless keyboards ______________________________
     ____

IV. Pointing devices [p. 4.7]
A pointing device is ______________________________
____
A pointer or mouse pointer is ______________________________

A. Mouse [p. 4.7]

A mouse is ____________________

____

1. Using a mouse [p. 4.8]

   As you move the mouse across a flat surface, the pointer on the screen also moves. When the pointer rests on an object, generally you press, or click, one of the mouse buttons to perform a certain action on that object.

2. Mouse types [p. 4.9]

   - A mechanical mouse has ____________________

     ____

   - An optical mouse has ____________________

     ____

   - A cordless mouse uses ____________________

     ____

B. Trackball [p. 4.10]

A trackball is ____________________

____

C. Touchpad [p. 4.11]

A touchpad or trackpad is ____________________

____

D. Pointing stick [p. 4.11]

A pointing stick is ____________________

____

E. Joystick [p. 4.12]

A joystick is ____________________

____

F. Touch screen [p. 4.12]

A touch screen is ____________________

____

G. Pen input [p. 4.12]

Pen input allows people to use an electronic pen, instead of a keyboard or mouse, for input.

1. Light pen [p. 4.12]

   A light pen is ____________________

   ____

2. Pen computing [p. 4.13]

   Pen computing lets people input data with an electronic pen (or stylus) that looks like a ballpoint pen but uses an electronic head instead of ink.

   Handwriting recognition software ______________________________

   ____

3. Graphics tablet [p. 4.13]

   A graphics table consists of ______________________________

   ____

V. Scanners and reading devices [p. 4.13]

A source document is ______________________________

Scanners and reading devices make the input process more efficient by capturing data directly from source documents.

A. Optical scanner [p. 4.14]

An optical scanner, or scanner, is ______________________________

____

When a document is scanned, the results are stored in rows and columns of dots called a bitmap. The resolution, or density of the dots, determines the sharpness and clarity of the image.

Resolution typically is measured in ______________________________

Image processing, or imaging, consists of ______________________________

____

B. Optical readers [p. 4.16]

An optical reader is ______________________________

____

1. Optical character recognition [p. 4.16]

   Optical character recognition (OCR) is ______________________________

   ____

   Optical character recognition (OCR) software ______________________________

   ____

2. Optical mark recognition [p. 4.17]

   Optical mark recognition (OMR) devices ______________________________

   ____

3. Bar code scanner [p. 4.17]

   A bar code scanner ______________________________

   ____

C. Magnetic ink character recognition reader [p. 4.19]

A magnetic ink character recognition (MICR) reader is____________________

____

D. Data collection devices [p. 4.20]

Data collection devices are ____

____

VI. Digital cameras [p. 4.20]

A digital camera ____

____

Basic types of digital cameras:

- Studio camera – ____
- Field camera – ____
- Point-and-shoot camera – ____

As with a scanner, the quality of a digital camera is measured by the number of bits it stores in a dot and the number of dots per inch, or resolution; the higher the numbers, the better the quality.

VII. Audio and video input [p. 4.22]

A. Audio input [p. 4.22]

Audio input is ____

Windows stores audio files as____

B. Speech recognition [p. 4.23]

Speech recognition (or voice recognition) is ____________________________

____

With speaker-dependent software____________________________________

____

Speaker-independent software ______________________________________

____

Discrete speech recognition software requires ___________________________

____

Continuous speech recognition software allows__________________________

____

C. Video input [p. 4.24]

Video input, or video capture, is_____________________________________

____

Like audio files, video files can require tremendous amounts of storage space.

The Moving Picture Experts Group (MPEG) ____________________________

____

A video digitizer ____

D. Videoconferencing [p. 4.25]

A videoconference is ____

____

A whiteboard ____

VIII. Input devices for physically challenged users [p. 4.26]

The Americans with Disabilities Act (ADA) requires ________________________

____

A keyguard ____

____

A head-mounted pointer is used to _____________________________________

____

Self Test

Matching

1. ____ mouse
2. ____ QWERTY keyboard
3. ____ trackball
4. ____ Dvorak keyboard
5. ____ touchpad
6. ____ enhanced keyboard
7. ____ pointing stick
8. ____ wireless keyboard
9. ____ joystick
10. ____ touch screen

a. monitor that has a touch-sensitive panel on the screen

b. light-sensing input device that reads printed text and graphics and then transmits the results into a form the computer can understand

c. keyboard with twelve function keys, two CTRL keys, two ALT keys, and arrow keys

d. provides multiple users with an area on which they can write or draw

e. pointing device consisting of a vertical lever resting on a base

f. pressure-sensitive pointing device shaped like a pencil eraser, developed by IBM

g. alternative keyboard layout that places often used letters in the middle of the typing area

h. standard computer keyboard named because of the layout of its typing area

i. small, flat, rectangular pointing device that is sensitive to pressure and motion

j. pointing device designed to fit comfortably under the palm of your hand

k. stationary pointing device with a ball mechanism on its top

l. keyboard that transmits data via infrared light waves

True/False

____ 1. Menu-driven programs use icons, buttons, and other graphical objects to issue commands.

____ 2. The command associated with a function key depends on the program you are using.

____ 3. The mouse is the most widely used pointing device because it takes full advantage of a graphical user interface.

____ 4. An optical mouse is less accurate than a mechanical mouse, but it also is less expensive.

____ 5. An advantage of using a pointing stick is that it does not require cleaning like a mouse or trackball.

____ 6. When an optical scanner is used, the fewer bits used to represent a dot, the more colors and shades of gray that can be represented.

____ 7. A sheet-fed scanner is similar to a copy machine, and is larger and more expensive than a flatbed scanner.

____ 8. MICR (magnetic-ink character recognition) is used almost exclusively by the banking industry for check processing.

____ 9. WAV files usually are small – requiring less than 1 KB of storage space for several minutes of audio.

____ 10. To participate in a videoconference, you must have a microphone, speakers, and a video camera mounted on your computer.

Multiple Choice

____ 1. What is a user response?
   a. a collection of unorganized facts
   b. a series of instructions that tells a computer how to perform tasks
   c. an instruction given to a computer program
   d. an instruction you issue to the computer by replying to a question

____ 2. In many programs, what function key can be pressed to display a Help window?
   a. F1
   b. F2
   c. F3
   d. F4

____ 3. What key is a toggle key that can be used to switch between two different states?
   a. PAGE UP
   b. NUM LOCK
   c. PRINT SCREEN
   d. BACKSPACE

____ 4. What is the most widely used pointing device?
   a. the touchpad
   b. the trackball
   c. the joystick
   d. the mouse

____ 5. In Windows 98, how do you display the Start menu on the screen?
   a. point at the Start button and drag the button onto the desktop
   b. point at the Start button and click the primary mouse button
   c. point at the Start button and right-click the secondary mouse button
   d. point at the Start button and double-click the primary mouse button

____ 6. What input device often is used in kiosks located in stores, hotels, airports, and museums?
   a. joysticks
   b. touch screens
   c. pointing sticks
   d. touchpads

____ 7. What device captures data directly from source documents?
   a. optical scanners
   b. bar code scanners
   c. magnetic-ink character recognition readers
   d. all of the above

____ 8. How would the resolution of a scanner with 1200 rows and 600 columns of dots be stated?
   a. 600 dpi
   b. 600 x 1200 dpi
   c. 1200 dpi
   d. 1200 x 600 dpi

____ 9. What type of bar code is used primarily in supermarkets, convenience, and specialty stores to identify manufacturers and products?
   a. UPC – Universal Product Code
   b. Codabar
   c. POSTNET – Postal Numeric Encoding Technique
   d. Interleaved 2 of 5

____ 10. What does an individual use to press the keys on a screen-displayed keyboard?
   a. a scanner
   b. a keyboard
   c. a pointing device
   d. a whiteboard

Fill in the Blanks

1. The ____________________, is a symbol that indicates where on the screen the next character you type will display.
2. The goal of ____________________ is to incorporate comfort, efficiency, and safety into the design of items in the workplace.
3. A mouse often rests on a(n) ____________________, which usually is a rectangular rubber or foam pad that provides better traction for the mouse.
4. You draw on a graphics tablet using a(n) ____________________, which is a device that looks similar to a mouse, except that it has a window with cross hairs so you can see through to the tablet.

5. Scanned documents can be stored and indexed using a(n) ____________________, which serves as an electronic filing cabinet that provides access to reproductions of the original documents.
6. Most ____________________ include a small optical scanner for reading characters and sophisticated software for analyzing what is read.
7. OCR frequently is used for ____________________ documents, which are documents designed to be returned to the organization that created and sent them.
8. A(n) ____________________ is an identification code that consists of a set of vertical lines and spaces of different widths.
9. With some digital cameras, you ____________________, or transfer a copy of, the stored pictures to your computer by connecting a cable between the digital camera and your computer using special software included with the camera.
10. To capture video, you plug a video camera, VCR, or other video device into a(n) ____________________, which is an expansion card that converts the analog video signal into a digital signal that a computer can understand.

Complete the Table

MOUSE OPERATIONS

Operation	Mouse Action
________________	Move the mouse across a flat surface until the pointer rests on the item of choice on the desktop.
________________	Press and release the primary mouse button, which usually is the left mouse button.
________________	Press and release the secondary mouse button, which usually is the right mouse button.
________________	Quickly press and release the primary mouse button twice without moving the mouse.
________________	Point to an item, hold down the primary mouse button, move the item, and then release the primary mouse button.
________________	Point to an item, hold down the secondary mouse button, move the item, and then release the secondary mouse button.
________________	Roll the wheel located between the two buttons forward or backward.
________________	Press the wheel button while moving the mouse on the desktop.

Things to Think About

1. Four types of input are data, programs, commands, and user responses. What type of input device (keyboard, pointing devices, scanners, and so on) can be used to enter each type of input?
2. How is a laptop computer keyboard different from a desktop computer keyboard? What keys might be left off of, or serve more than one purpose on, a laptop keyboard?
3. What pointing device would you most like to have with a desktop computer? What pointing device would you most like to have with a laptop computer? Why?
4. How do scanners and reading devices make the input process more efficient and accurate? For what, if any, types of input are scanners and reading devices unsuitable? Why?

Puzzle

The terms described by the phrases below are written below each line in code. Break the code by writing the correct term above the coded word. Then, use your broken code to translate the final sentence.

1. the most commonly used input device — PVBYLZIW
2. allows users to touch areas of the screen to enter data — GLFXS HXIVVM
3. vertical lines and spaces of different widths — YZI XLWVH
4. type of documents designed to be returned — GFIM-ZILFMW
5. on-screen symbol usually represented by an arrow-shape — KLRMGVI
6. can capture and save an individual frame from a video — ERWVL WRTRGRAVI
7. calculator-style arrangement of keys on a computer keyboard — MFNVIRX PVBKZW
8. data or instructions entered into the memory of a computer — RMKFG
9. indicates where the next character typed will appear — RMHVIGRLM KLRMG
10. keys that move the insertion point — ZIILD PVBH
11. keys that can be switched between two different states — GLTTOV PVBH
12. allows you to take and store photographic images digitally — WRTRGZO XZNVIZ
13. collection of unorganized facts — WZGZ
14. meeting between people who use a network or the Internet — ERWVLXLMUVIVMXV
15. original form of data captured with scanners — HLFIXV WLXFNVMG
16. similar to a copy machine except that it creates a document file — HXZMMVI

17. determines the sharpness and clearness of a scanned image — ________________ IVHLOFGRLM
18. input device often used with computer games — ________________ QLBHGRXP
19. the way Windows stores audio files — ________________ DZEVULINH
20. type of program that uses lists as a means to enter commands — ________________ NVMF-WIREVM

____

GBKRHGH FHRMT GSV NLOGILM PVBYLZIW, DSRXS RH HKORG ZMW

____

XLMGLFIVW GL URG VZXS SZMW DRGS GSV NLHG XLNNLMOB FHVW PVBH

____

FMWVI GSV HGILMTVHG URMTVIH, XZM GBKV NLIV GSZM GSIVV GRNVH

____

UZHGVI GSZM GBKRHGH FHRMT Z GIZWRGRLMZO PVBYLZIW.

Self Test Answers

Matching

1. *j* [p. 4.7]
2. *h* [p. 4.6]
3. *k* [p. 4.10]
4. *g* [p. 4.6]
5. *i* [p. 4.11]
6. *c* [p. 4.6]
7. *f* [p. 4.11]
8. *l* [p. 4.6]
9. *e* [p. 4.12]
0. *a* [p. 4.12]

True/False

1. *F* [p. 4.3]
2. *T* [p. 4.4]
3. *T* [p. 4.7]
4. *F* [p. 4.9]
5. *T* [p. 4.11]
6. *F* [p. 4.14]
7. *F* [p. 4.15]
8. *T* [p. 4.19]
9. *F* [p. 4.22]
0. *T* [p. 4.25]

Multiple Choice

1. *d* [p. 4.3]
2. *a* [p. 4.4]
3. *b* [p. 4.5]
4. *d* [p. 4.7]
5. *b* [p. 4.8]
6. *b* [p. 4.12]
7. *d* [p. 4.13]
8. *b* [p. 4.15]
9. *a* [p. 4.18]
0. *c* [p. 4.26]

Fill in the Blanks

1. *insertion point* [p. 4.5]
2. *ergonomics* [p. 4.6]
3. *mouse pad* [p. 4.7]
4. *puck* [p. 4.13]
5. *image processing system* [p. 4.16]
6. *OCR devices* [p. 4.16]
7. *turn-around* [p. 4.16]
8. *bar code* [p. 4.17]
9. *download* [p. 4.20]
0. *video capture card* [p. 4.24]

Complete the Table

MOUSE OPERATIONS

Operation	Mouse Action
Point	Move the mouse across a flat surface until the pointer rests on the item of choice on the desktop.
Click	Press and release the primary mouse button, which usually is the left mouse button.
Right-click	Press and release the secondary mouse button, which usually is the right mouse button.
Double-click	Quickly press and release the primary mouse button twice without moving the mouse.
Drag	Point to an item, hold down the primary mouse button, move the item, and then release the primary mouse button.
Right-drag	Point to an item, hold down the secondary mouse button, move the item, and then release the secondary mouse button.

Operation	Mouse Action
Rotate wheel	Roll the wheel located between the two buttons forward or backward.
Press wheel button	Press the wheel button while moving the mouse on the desktop.

Things to Think About

Answers will vary.

Puzzle Answer

	Clue	Answer
1.	the most commonly used input device	*keyboard* PVBYLZIW
2.	allows users to touch areas of the screen to enter data	*touch screen* GLFXS HXIVVM
3.	vertical lines and spaces of different widths	*bar code* YZI XLWVH
4.	type of documents designed to be returned	*turn-around* GFIM-ZILFMW
5.	on-screen symbol usually represented by an arrow-shape	*pointer* KLRMGVI
6.	can capture and save an individual frame from a video	*video digitizer* ERWVL WRTRGRAVI
7.	calculator-style arrangement of keys on a computer keyboard	*numeric keypad* MFNVIRX PVBKZW
8.	data or instructions entered into the memory of a computer	*input* RMKFG
9.	indicates where the next character typed will appear	*insertion point* RMHVIGRLM KLRMG
10.	keys that move the insertion point	*arrow keys* ZIILD PVBH
11.	keys that can be switched between two different states	*toggle keys* GLTTOV PVBH
12.	allows you to take and store photographic images digitally	*digital camera* WRTRGZO XZNVIZ

13. collection of unorganized facts — *data*
WZGZ

14. meeting between people who use a network or the Internet — *videoconference*
ERWVLXLMUVIVMXV

15. original form of data captured with scanners — *source document*
HLFIXV WLXFNVMG

16. similar to a copy machine except that it creates a document file — *scanner*
HXZMMVI

17. determines the sharpness and clearness of a scanned image — *resolution*
IVHLOFGRLM

18. input device often used with computer games — *joystick*
QLBHGRXP

19. the way Windows stores audio files — *waveforms*
DZEVULINH

20. type of program that uses lists as a means to enter commands — *menu-driven*
NVMF-WIREVM

Typists using the Moltron keyboard, which is split and
GBKRHGH FHRMT GSV NLOGILM PVBYLZIW, DSRXS RH HKORG ZMW

contoured to fit each hand with the most commonly used keys
XLMGLFIVW GL URG VZXS SZMW DRGS GSV NLHG XLNNLMOB FHVW PVBH

under the strongest fingers, can type more than three times
FMWVI GSV HGILMTVHG URMTVIH, XZM GBKV NLIV GSZM GSIVV GRNVH

faster than typists using a traditional keyboard.
UZHGVI GSZM GBKRHGH FHRMT Z GIZWRGRLMZO PVBYLZIW.

DISCOVERING COMPUTERS 2000

STUDY GUIDE

CHAPTER 5

Output

Chapter Overview

In this chapter, you learn what is output and what are output devices. Display devices are introduced, including CRT monitors, flat-panel displays, video cards, and high-definition television. You explore monitor quality and monitor ergonomics. Various types of printers are presented, such as impact printers, nonimpact printers, portable printers, plotters and large-format printers, and special-purpose printers. You find out about audio output and other output devices, including data projectors, facsimile machines, and multifunction devices. Finally, you become acquainted with terminals and output devices for physically challenged users.

Chapter Objectives

After completing this chapter, you should be able to:

- Define the four types of output
- Identify the different types of display devices
- Describe factors that affect the quality of a monitor
- Understand the purpose of a video card
- Identify monitor ergonomic issues
- Explain the differences among various types of printers
- List various types of audio output devices
- Identify the purpose of data projectors, fax machines, and multifunction devices
- Explain how a terminal is both an input and output device
- Identify output options for physically challenged users

Chapter Outline

I. What is output? [p. 5.2]

Output is ______________________________

____

Common types of output:

- Text consists of ______________________________

  ____

- Graphics are ______________________________

  ____

- Audio is ______________________________

  ____

- Video consists of ______________________________

  ____

II. What are output devices? [p. 5.3]

An output device is ______________________________

____

III. Display devices [p. 5.3]

A display device is ______________________________

____

A. CRT monitors [p. 5.3]

A CRT monitor, or monitor, is ______________________________

____

- A color monitor ______________________________

  ____

- A monochrome monitor ______________________________

  ____

The core of a CRT monitor is a large glass tube called a cathode ray tube (CRT). The screen, which is the front of the tube, is coated with tiny dots of phosphor material that glow when electrically charged. Each dot, called a pixel, is a single point in an electronic image.

Most monitors are referred to by their viewable size, which is ____________

____

B. Flat-panel displays [p. 5.4]

A flat-panel display is ______________________________

____

1. LCD displays [p. 5.4]

A liquid crystal display (LCD) ______________________________

____

- An active-matrix display ______________________________

  ____

- A passive-matrix display ______________________________

  ____

2. Gas plasma monitors [p. 5.6]

   Gas plasma monitors ____

   ____

C. Monitor quality [p. 5.6]

   The quality of a monitor's display depends largely on its resolution, dot pitch, and refresh rate.

   Resolution, or sharpness and clarity, is ____

   ____

   Dot pitch is ____

   Refresh rate is ____

D. Video cards [p. 5.8]

   A video card converts ____

   ____

   Today, just about every monitor supports the ____

   ______________________________ standard.

   Video RAM (VRAM) is ____

E. Monitor ergonomics [p. 5.10]

   To address ergonomic issues, many monitors have controls that allow you to adjust the brightness, contrast, positioning, height, and width of images.

   Monitors produce a small amount of electromagnetic radiation (EMR), which is ____

   The ENERGY STAR program, developed by the U.S. Department of Energy and the U.S. Environmental Protection Agency, encourages ______________

   ____

F. High-definition television [p. 5.11]

   High-definition television (HDTV) is ____

   ____

IV. Printers [p. 5.11]

   A printer is ____

   ____

   - Portrait orientation is ____
   - Landscape orientation is ____

A. Impact printers [p. 5.12]

   An impact printer ____

   ____

1. Dot-matrix printers [p. 5.12]

   A dot-matrix printer is ______________________________

   ____

   Most dot-matrix printers use ______________________________

   ____

   The speed of dot-matrix printers is measured in ______________

2. Line printers [p. 5.13]

   A line printer is ______________________________

   ____

   - A band printer ______________________________

     ____

   - A shuttle-matrix printer ______________________________

     ____

B. Nonimpact printers [p. 5.14]

A nonimpact printer ______________________________

____

1. Ink-jet printers [p. 5.14]

   An ink-jet printer is ______________________________

   ____

   Ink-jet printer resolution is measured by ______________

   ____

   Ink-jet printer speed is measured by ______________________

2. Laser printers [p. 5.16]

   A laser printer is ______________________________

   ____

   A page description language (PDL) ______________________

   ____

   Operating in a manner similar to a copy machine, a laser printer creates images using a laser beam and toner, which is ______________

   ____

3. Thermal printers [p. 5.17]

   A thermal printer ______________________________

   ____

   - A thermal wax-transfer printer ______________________

     ____

- A dye-sublimation printer ______________________________

____

C. Portable printers [p. 5.18]

A portable printer is ______________________________

____

D. Plotters and large-format printers [p. 5.19]

Plotters and large format printers are sophisticated printers used to produce high-quality drawings.

- A pen plotter ______________________________

  ____

- An electrostatic plotter ______________________________

  ____

- A large-format printer ______________________________

  ____

E. Special-purpose printers [p. 5.20]

A snapshot printer is ______________________________

____

A label printer is ______________________________

____

V. Audio output [p. 5.20]

Audio output devices are ______________________________

____

Although most PCs have a small internal speaker that outputs low-quality sound, many computer users add higher-quality stereo speakers to their computers. With a headset, ______________________________

VI. Other output devices [p. 5.21]

A. Data projectors [p. 5.21]

A data projector ______________________________

____

- An LCD projector ______________________________

  ____

- A digital light processing (DLP) projector ______________________________

  ____

B. Facsimile (fax) machine [p. 5.22]

A facsimile (fax) machine is ______________________________

____

A fax modem is ______________________________

____

C. Multifunction devices [p. 5.23]

A multifunction device (MFD) is ______________________________

____

VII. Terminals [p. 5.23]

A terminal is ______________________________

____

- A dumb terminal ______________________________

  ____

- An intelligent terminal ______________________________

  ____

Special purpose terminals:

- A point-of-sale (POS) terminal ______________________________

  ____

- An automatic teller machine (ATM) is ______________________________

  ____

VIII. Output devices for physically challenged users [p. 5.24]

With Windows, users can set options in the Accessibility Properties dialog box to

____

A Braille printer ______________________________

Self Test

Matching

1. ____ dot-matrix printer
2. ____ band printer
3. ____ shuttle-matrix printer
4. ____ ink-jet printer
5. ____ laser printer
6. ____ thermal printer
7. ____ portable printer
8. ____ large-format printer
9. ____ snapshot printer
10. ____ label printer

a. small, lightweight printer used with a laptop or handheld computer
b. uses a row of charged wires to draw an electrostatic pattern on specially coated paper
c. generates images by pushing electrically heated pins against heat-sensitive paper
d. impact printer that produces images when tiny wire pins strike an inked ribbon
e. high-speed, high-quality nonimpact printer that works in a manner similar to a copy machine
f. prints fully-formed characters when hammers strike a rotating band
g. used by graphic artists to create photo-realistic quality color prints
h. uses one or more colored pens or a scribing device to draw on paper or transparencies
i. produces photo lab quality pictures from images scanned or taken with a digital camera
j. nonimpact printer that forms characters and graphics by spraying tiny drops of liquid ink
k. small printer that prints on an adhesive-type material that can be placed on items
l. moves a series of print hammers back and forth horizontally at incredibly high speeds

True/False

____ 1. Color monitors are rarely used because most of today's software is not designed to display information in color.

____ 2. Unlike a CRT monitor, an LCD display does not use a cathode ray tube to create images on the screen.

____ 3. A monitor with a lower resolution displays a greater number of pixels, which provides a smoother image.

____ 4. The number of colors that a video card can display is determined by the number of bits it uses to store information about each pixel.

____ 5. Many programs can be broadcast on a single analog channel, whereas only one program can be broadcast on a digital channel.

____ 6. Letter quality (LQ) output is a quality of print acceptable for business letters.

____ 7. With an ink-jet printer, the smaller the dpi (dots per inch), the better the quality of the image.

____ 8. PostScript, a page description language, is used in fields such as desktop publishing and graphic art because it is designed for complex documents with intense graphics and colors.

____ 9. When using a headset, anyone within listening distance can hear the output.

____ 10. Small offices and home offices use multifunction devices because they take up less space than a separate printer, scanner, copy machine, and fax machine.

Multiple Choice

____ 1. Image editing software allows you to alter what type of output by including enhancements such as blended colors, animation, and other special effects?
   a. text
   b. graphics
   c. audio
   d. video

____ 2. How is the viewable size of most monitors measured?
   a. in square inches, stating the area of the screen on the front of the cathode ray tube
   b. vertically, from the top left corner to the bottom left corner of the cathode ray tube
   c. horizontally, from the top left corner to the top left corner of the cathode ray tube
   d. diagonally, from a top corner to the opposite bottom corner of the cathode ray tube

____ 3. A color monitor separates a video signal into what colors?
   a. green, yellow, and blue
   b. blue, yellow, and red
   c. yellow, red, and green
   d. red, green, and blue

____ 4. What type of memory do higher-quality video cards use to improve the quality of graphics?
   a. video RAM or VRAM
   b. dynamic RAM or DRAM
   c. video ROM or VROM
   d. dynamic ROM or DROM

____ 5. Which of the following is *not* a commonly used type of nonimpact printer?
   a. dot-matrix printers
   b. ink-jet printers
   c. laser printers
   d. thermal printers

____ 6. Because of its reasonable cost and letter-quality print, what type of printer has become the most popular type of printer for use in the home?
   a. laser printers
   b. dot-matrix printers
   c. thermal printers
   d. ink-jet printers

____ 7. How is the speed of ink-jet printers measured?
   a. characters per second (cps)
   b. dots per inch (dpi)
   c. pages per minute (ppm)
   d. lines per minute (lpm)

____ 8. How do pen plotters differ from other printers?
   a. they generate lines by printing closely spaced dots, whereas most printers produce continuous lines
   b. they produce continuous lines, whereas most printers generate lines by printing closely spaced dots
   c. they form characters and graphics without striking the paper, whereas most printers have a print mechanism that physically contacts the paper
   d. they have a print mechanism that physically contacts the paper, whereas most printers form characters and graphics without striking the paper

____ 9. What type of smaller, lower-cost data projector uses tiny mirrors to reflect light, producing crisp, bright, colorful images that remain in focus and can be seen clearly even in a well-lit room?
   a. an LCD projector
   b. a large-format projector
   c. a digital light processing (DLP) projector
   d. an electrostatic projector

____ 10. What can people use to instruct the Windows operating system to display visual signals in situations where normally it would make a sound?
   a. the Accessibility Properties dialog box
   b. the System Properties dialog box
   c. the Power Management Properties dialog box
   d. the Sounds Properties dialog box

Fill in the Blanks

1. A(n) ____________________ is a letter, number, punctuation mark, or any other symbol that requires one byte of computer storage space.

2. Some monochrome monitors use ____________________, which enhances the quality of their graphics display by using many shades of gray to form images.
3. Refresh rate is measured according to ____________________, which is the number of times per second the screen is redrawn.
4. With a technique called ____________________, some older monitors refresh images by using the electron beam to draw only half the horizontal line with each pass.
5. Hard copy, also called a(n) ____________________, can be printed in portrait or landscape orientation.
6. Most dot-matrix printers use ____________________, in which each sheet of paper is connected together.
7. Because they process and store an entire page before they print it, laser printers sometimes are called ____________________.
8. A(n) ____________________ tells a laser printer how to layout the contents of a printed page.
9. Laser printers create an image using a laser beam and powdered ink, called ____________________, which is packaged in a cartridge.
10. Intelligent terminals sometimes are called ____________________ because they can be programmed by the software developer to perform basic tasks.

Complete the Table

VIDEO STANDARDS

Standard	Suggested Resolution	Possible Simultaneous Colors
Monochrome Display Adapter (MDA)	720 x 350	____________
____________________	640 x 480	____________
	320 x 200	256
Extended Graphics Array (XGA)	1024 x 768	____________
	____________	65,536
____________________	800 x 600	____________
	1280 x 1024	____________

Things to Think About

1. Why is output printed on paper, which is a flexible material, called hard copy while output displayed on a screen, which is firm to the touch, called soft copy?

2. What advantages do LCD displays offer over CRT monitors? Will LCD displays someday replace CRT monitors? Why or why not?
3. Using Figure 5-18 (page 5.12), answer each question about your current printer requirements. Based on your answers, what type of printer would you be most likely to buy? Why?
4. How important is audio? Would you consider adding higher-quality stereo speakers, a woofer, or a headset to your personal computer? Why or why not?

Puzzle

All of the words described below appear in the puzzle. Words may be either forward or backward, across, up and down, or diagonal. Circle each word as you find it.

Output

```
        M
      R C D
    T E H B M
  O C T A M P Q
W X F N R X P O J
    Q I A Q O
  A I R C U R E
M L G P T R T E I
T D P O P E A R L D G
  W U I R T A A
S T D H D A I N D
S R E S O L U T I O N
H D C E O C T P A M M F U
R P F H I P D R L
F H A T R R H I E Z K
E A E C C U E G P T L D P
R H G R S O O M N M A C C I Z
V T D P S E F O L R H
A S Z N Y C D D W T E G S
K O H L A T R O T I N O M Y H
F P I X E L J E M T C V H J I Z G
        E X K
        N A T
        U F G
```

data that has been processed into a useful form

characters used to create words, sentences, and paragraphs

letter, number, or other symbol requiring one byte of storage space

digital representation of nontext information

music, speech, or any other sound

images played back at speeds that provide the appearance of motion

information shown on a display device

display device consisting of a screen housed in a plastic or metal case

front of a cathode ray tube

single point in an electronic image

type of display that does not use CRT

sharpness or clarity of a monitor

vertical distance between pixels on a monitor

speed with which the monitor redraws images on the screen

measure of refresh rate

converts digital output into an analog signal

standard supported today by just about every monitor

output device that produces text and graphics on a physical medium

orientation taller than it is wide

orientation wider than it is tall

unit in which dot-matrix printer speed is measured

unit in which ink-jet printer resolution is measured

unit in which ink-jet printer speed is measured

tells a laser printer how to layout a page

page description language commonly used in desktop publishing

powdered ink used by laser printers

communications device that transmits computer-prepared documents

single piece of equipment that provides the functionality of a printer, scanner, and copy machine

device that performs both input and output

self-service banking machine

Self Test Answers

Matching

1. *d* [p. 5.12]
2. *f* [p. 5.13]
3. *l* [p. 5.13]
4. *j* [p. 5.14]
5. *e* [p. 5.16]
6. *c* [p. 5.17]
7. *a* [p. 5.18]
8. *g* [p. 5.19]
9. *i* [p. 5.20]
0. *k* [p. 5.20]

True/False

1. *F* [p. 5.3]
2. *T* [p. 5.5]
3. *F* [p. 5.7]
4. *T* [p. 5.8]
5. *F* [p. 5.11]
6. *T* [p. 5.12]
7. *F* [p. 5.14]
8. *T* [p. 5.16]
9. *F* [p. 5.21]
0. *T* [p. 5.23]

Multiple Choice

1. *b* [p. 5.2]
2. *d* [p. 5.4]
3. *d* [p. 5.8]
4. *a* [p. 5.9]
5. *a* [p. 5.14]
6. *d* [p. 5.14]
7. *c* [p. 5.15]
8. *b* [p. 5.19]
9. *c* [p. 5.21]
0. *a* [p. 5.24]

Fill in the Blanks

1. *character* [p. 5.2]
2. *gray scaling* [p. 5.3]
3. *hertz* [p. 5.7]
4. *interlacing* [p. 5.7]
5. *printout* [p. 5.11]
6. *continuous-form paper* [p. 5.13]
7. *page printers* [p. 5.16]
8. *page description language (PDL)* [p. 5.16]
9. *toner* [p. 5.17]
0. *programmable terminals* [p. 5.23]

Complete the Table

VIDEO STANDARDS

Standard	Suggested Resolution	Possible Simultaneous Colors
Monochrome Display Adapter (MDA)	720 x 350	*1*
Video Graphics Array (VGA)	640 x 480	*16*
	320 x 200	256
Extended Graphics Array (XGA)	1024 x 768	*256*
	640 x 480	65,536
Super Video Graphics Array (SVGA)	800 x 600	*16 million*
	1280 x 1024	*16 million*

Things to Think About

Answers will vary.

Puzzle Answer

Output

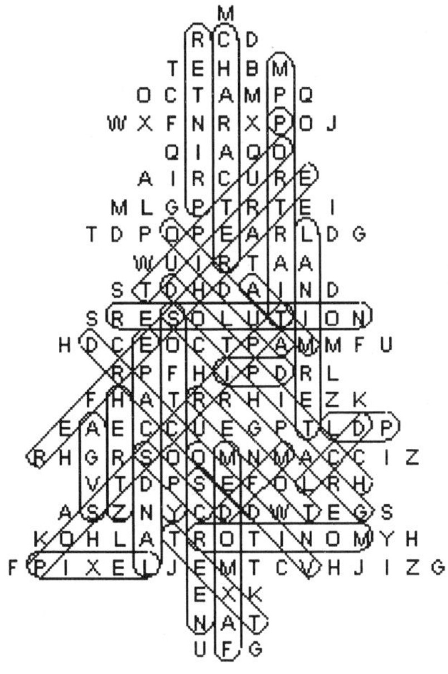

DISCOVERING COMPUTERS 2000

STUDY GUIDE

CHAPTER 6

Storage

Chapter Overview

This chapter explains various storage media and storage devices. You discover how memory is different from storage. Floppy disks are introduced, and characteristics of a floppy disk, floppy disk drives, care of floppy disks, and high-capacity floppy disks are presented. Hard disks are explained, and you find out about characteristics of a hard disk, how a hard disk works, removable hard disks, hard disk controllers, RAID, and maintaining data on a hard disk. Compact discs, including CD-ROMs and DVD-ROMs, are described. Finally, you learn about tapes, PC Cards, and other types of storage such as smart cards, microfilm and microfiche.

Chapter Objectives

After completing this chapter, you should be able to:

- ◆ Differentiate between storage and memory
- ◆ Identify various types of storage media and storage devices
- ◆ Explain how data is stored on a floppy disk
- ◆ Understand how to care for a floppy disk
- ◆ Describe how a hard disk organizes data
- ◆ List the advantages of using disks
- ◆ Explain how data is stored on compact discs
- ◆ Understand how to care for a compact disc
- ◆ Differentiate between CD-ROMs and DVD-ROMs
- ◆ Identify uses of tapes, PC Cards, smart cards, microfilm, and microfiche

CHAPTER OUTLINE

I. Memory versus storage [p. 6.2]

A. Memory [p. 6.2]

Memory, which is composed of one or more chips on the motherboard, holds data and instructions while they are being processed by the CPU.

Types of memory:

- The contents of volatile memory ______________________________

____

- The contents of nonvolatile memory ______________________________

B. Storage [p. 6.2]

Storage ______________________________

A storage medium is ______________________________

A storage device is ______________________________

Storage devices function as sources of both input and output.

- Reading is ______________________________
- Writing is ______________________________

Access time is ______________________________

Capacity is ______________________________

II. Floppy disks [p. 6.4]

A floppy disk is ______________________________

A. Characteristics of a floppy disk [p. 6.5]

Magnetic disks are read/write storage media, meaning that you can read (access) data from and write (place) data on a magnetic disk any number of times.

Formatting is ______________________________

- A track is ______________________________
- A sector is ______________________________
- A cluster is ______________________________

Disk density determines a disk's storage capacity; the higher the density, the larger the storage capacity.

Today, most floppy disks are high density, storing _________ MB of data.

The file allocation table (FAT) ______________________________

A write-protect notch is ______________________________

B. Floppy disk drives [p. 6.7]

A floppy disk drive (FDD) is ______________________________

____

To read from or write on a floppy disk, the floppy disk drive must support the floppy disk's density.

When you insert a floppy disk into a floppy disk drive, the drive slides the shutter (a metal cover over an opening in the disk's plastic shell) to the side to expose a portion of the recording surface.

The read/write head ______________________________

____

C. Care of floppy disks [p. 6.9]

When handling a floppy disk, avoid ______________________________

____

D. High-capacity floppy disks [p. 6.9]

High-capacity disks can store ______________________________

____

A backup is ______________________________

High-capacity disk drives:

- SuperDisk™ drive ______________________________
- HiFD (High FD) ______________________________
- Zip® drive ______________________________

III. Hard disks [p. 6.10]

Hard disks provide far larger storage capacities and much faster access times than floppy disks and are the primary media for storing software programs and files.

A hard disk ______________________________

____

A platter ______________________________

____

A. Characteristics of a hard disk [p. 6.11]

Hard disks undergo two formatting steps:

- A low-level format ______________________________

  ____

  After low-level formatting, a hard disk can be divided into partitions, or separate areas that function as separate hard disks. Partitioning makes a hard disk more efficient or allows for the installation of multiple operating systems.

- A high-level format ____

B. How a hard disk works [p. 6.12]

Most hard disks have multiple platters, stacked on top of one another, each of which has a read/write head for each side.

A cylinder is ____

The platters spin continually at a high rate of speed, with the read/write heads floating on a cushion of air just above the platter surface.

A head crash ____

Access time for hard disks is faster than for floppy disks because:

(1) ____

(2) ____

Disk cache is ____

C. Removable hard disks [p. 6.14]

A removable hard disk or disk cartridge is ____

The Jaz® disk ____

Advantages of portable media over fixed disks: ____

A disk pack ____

D. Hard disk controllers [p. 6.14]

A disk controller is a special-purpose chip and its associated electronic circuits that manages the flow of data, instructions, and information to and from a disk.

A hard disk controller (HDC) ____

Two types of controllers for PCs are EIDE and SCSI.

1. EIDE [p. 6.14]

   EIDE (Electronic Integrated Drive Electronics ____

2. SCSI [p. 6.14]

   SCSI (Small computer system interface) ____

E. RAID [p. 6.15]

RAID (redundant array of independent disks) ______________________

____

RAID is used with network and Internet servers. RAID improves reliability through the duplication of data, instructions, and information. Duplication is implemented in different way, depending on the storage design, or level, used.

- Mirroring (level 1) ______________________
- Striping ______________________

F. Maintaining data stored on a hard disk [p. 6.16]

To prevent loss of data, you should perform preventative maintenance such as

____

IV. Compact discs [p. 6.16]

A compact disc (CD) is ______________________

____

CDs store items using microscopic pits (indentations) and land (flat areas) in a single, spiral track. A high-powered laser light creates the pits, and a lower-powered laser reads items by reflecting light through the disc. The reflected light is converted into a series of bits that the computer can process.

A jewel box ______________________

Guidelines for proper care of CDs: ______________________

____

____

____

____

____

A. CD-ROMs [p. 6.19]

A CD-ROM is ______________________

____

The contents of a standard CD-ROM are recorded by the manufacturer and cannot be erased or modified.

A CD-ROM drive or CD-ROM player reads items on a CD-ROM.

A CD-ROM can hold ______________________

1. CD-ROM drive speed [p. 6.21]

Data transfer rate ______________________

____

CD-ROM drives use an X to denote the original data transfer rate of 150 KB per second. A 16X CD-ROM drive has a data transfer rate of 2,400 (16 x 150) KB per second. The higher the data transfer rate, the smoother the playback of images and sounds.

2. CD-ROM variations [p. 6.21]

   Most standard CD-ROMs are single-session, because all items must be written when the disc is manufactured. Some CD-ROM variations are multisession, meaning that additional data, instruction, and information can be written to the disc at a later time:

   - PhotoCD is ______________________________
     ____
   - CD-R (compact disc-recordable) is ______________________________
     ____
   - CD-RW (compact disc-rewritable) is ______________________________
     ____

B. DVD-ROMs [p. 6.22]

A DVD-ROM (digital video disc-ROM) is ______________________________

____

DVD-ROMs increase storage capacity using one of three storage techniques:

____

____

____

1. DVD variations [p. 6.23]

   ____

   ____

   ____

V. Tapes [p. 6.23]

Magnetic tape ______________________________

____

- Tape storage requires sequential access, which refers to ______________________________
  ____
- Floppy disks, hard disks, and compact discs all use direct access or random access, which means ______________________________
  ____

A tape drive is ______________________________

A tape cartridge is ______________________________

Tape cartridges frequently are used for ______________________________

VI. PC Cards [p. 6.24]

A PC Card is ______________________________

____

Picture cards, or compact flash cards, ______________________________

____

VII. Other types of storage [p. 6.25]

A. Smart cards [p. 6.25]

A smart card ______________________________

____

Types of smart cards:

- An intelligent smart card ______________________________
- A memory card ______________________________

Smart cards store patient records, track information (such as purchases or attendance), or store prepaid amounts (as in a prepaid telephone card or electronic money).

Electronic money is ______________________________

B. Microfilm and microfiche [p. 6.26]

Microfilm and microfiche store microscopic images of documents.

Microfilm ______________________________

Microfiche ______________________________

Applications of microfilm and microfiche include ______________________________

____

Self Test

Matching

1. ____ floppy disk
2. ____ hard disk
3. ____ RAID
4. ____ CD-ROM
5. ____ DVD-ROM
6. ____ magnetic tape
7. ____ PC Card
8. ____ smart card
9. ____ microfilm
10. ____ microfiche

a. extremely high-capacity compact disc capable of storing from 4.7 GB to 17 GB

b. uses a small sheet of film to store microscopic images of documents

c. portable, inexpensive, flexible magnetic disk enclosed in a square-shaped plastic shell

d. magnetically coated ribbon capable of storing large amounts at a low cost

e. stores data on a thin microprocessor embedded in a card the size of a credit card

f. consists of several inflexible, circular platters on which items are stored electronically

g. a thin, credit-card sized device that fits into an expansion slot on a personal computer

h. sequential access storage medium whose contents are lost when power is turned off

i. a group of two or more integrated hard disks, usually more reliable than traditional disks

j. uses a 100- to 215-foot roll of film to store microscopic images of documents

k. temporarily holds data and instructions while they are being processed by the CPU

l. silver-colored compact disc that uses the same laser technology used for recording music

True/False

____ 1. Storage, also called secondary storage, auxiliary storage, or mass storage, holds items such as data, instructions, and information for future use.

____ 2. Even if a file consists of only a few bytes, an entire cluster of the floppy disk is used for storage.

____ 3. On a floppy disk, if the write-protect notch is exposed, or open, the drive can write on the floppy disk.

____ 4. A Macintosh computer can use a PC formatted disk without special equipment or software.

____ 5. Current personal computer hard disks can store from 2 to 16 GB of data, instructions, and information.

____ 6. If a hard disk has only one partition, the hard disk usually is called, or designated, drive A.

____ 7. Most manufacturers guarantee their hard disks to last somewhere between three and five years, although many last much longer with proper care.

____ 8. Like an audio CD, a CD-ROM cannot contain text, graphics, or video.

____ 9. Because sequential access is much slower than direct access, magnetic tapes no longer are used as a primary method of storage.

____ 10. Different types and sizes of PC Cards are used to add storage, additional memory, communications, and sound capabilities to a computer.

Multiple Choice

____ 1. How much data can a typical floppy disk store?
   a. 1.44 KB (approximately 1,440 bytes)
   b. 1.44 MB (approximately 1,440,000 bytes)
   c. 1.44 GB (approximately 1,440,000,000 bytes)
   d. 1.44 TB (approximately 1,440,000,000,000 bytes)

____ 2. What is the smallest unit of space used to store data?
   a. a track
   b. a sector
   c. a cluster
   d. a cylinder

____ 3. If a computer has one floppy disk drive, what is that drive usually designated?
   a. drive A
   b. drive B
   c. drive C
   d. drive D

____ 4. What should you do to promote the longevity of a floppy disk?
   a. expose the disk to excessive heat, sunlight, or cold
   b. place the disk near magnetic fields
   c. open the disk's shutter or touch the recording surface
   d. keep the disk in a storage tray when not in use

____ 5. What contaminant on a hard disk surface could cause a head crash and make the hard disk drive unusable?
   a. a hair
   b. dust
   c. smoke
   d. all of the above

____ 6. What popular, reasonably priced, removable hard disk by Iomega can store up to two gigabytes (GB) of data?
   a. SuperDisk™ disk
   b. HiFD disk
   c. Zip® disk
   d. Jaz® disk

____ 7. What Windows utility frees up space on a hard disk by listing files that can be deleted safely?
   a. Disk Defragmenter
   b. Disk Cleanup
   c. Compression Agent
   d. Resource Meter

____ 8. What should you do to care properly for a compact disc?
   a. hold the disc by its edges
   b. stack discs
   c. touch the underside of the disc
   d. write on the label side of the disc

____ 9. What speed CD-ROM would have a data transfer rate of 2,400 KB or 2.4 MB per second?
   a. 8X
   b. 16X
   c. 32X
   d. 40X

____ 10. What do libraries use to store back issues of newspapers, magazines, and genealogy records?
   a. floppy disks and hard disks
   b. CD-ROMs and DVD-ROMs
   c. PC Cards and smart cards
   d. microfilm and microfiche

Fill in the Blanks

1. One commonly used storage medium is a(n) ____________________, which is a round, flat piece of metal or plastic with a magnetic coating on which items can be written.

2. ____________________ is the process of preparing a disk (floppy or hard disk) for reading and writing by organizing the disk into storage locations.

3. A(n) ____________________ is a small opening at the corner of a floppy disk that protects the disk from being accidentally erased.

4. A(n) ____________________ is a duplicate of a file, program, or disk that can be used if the original is lost, damaged, or destroyed.

5. A(n) ____________________ occurs when a read/write head touches the surface of a hard disk platter, usually resulting in a loss of data or sometimes loss of the entire drive.
6. EIDE controllers also are referred to as the ____________________ that integrates the controller into the disk drive.
7. A protective case, called a(n) ____________________, protects data of any type on a compact disc.
8. CD-ROM is an abbreviation for ____________________.
9. ____________________ are a thicker type of PC Card used to house hard disks and currently have storage capacities of more than 520 MB.
10. A(n) ____________________ is used to record images onto microfilm or microfiche.

Complete the Table

3.5-INCH FLOPPY DISK DENSITIES

	Double Density (DD)	**High Density (HD)**
Capacity	____________	____________
Number of sides	2	2
Number of tracks	80	____________
Sectors per track	____________	____________
Bytes per sector	____________	512
Sectors per disk	____________	____________

Things to Think About

1. How is downward compatible different from upward compatible? Why are floppy disk drives downward compatible but not upward compatible?
2. How does partitioning make hard disks more efficient?
3. How is an EIDE controller different from a SCSI controller? When would each controller be used?
4. Will compact discs, such as CD-ROMs or DVD-ROMs, someday replace magnetic tape, microfilm, or microfiche? Why or why not?

Puzzle

Use the given clues to complete the crossword puzzle.

Storage

Across

1. Extremely high capacity compact disc
4. Minimum time it takes a storage device to locate an item on a disk
8. A group of two or more integrated hard disks
9. RAID storage design that splits items across multiple disks in the array
11. Narrow recording band that forms a full circle on a disk surface
15. Separate areas into which a hard disk can be divided, each of which functions as a separate hard disk drive
17. Portable, inexpensive storage medium
18. Small arcs into which a disk's tracks are broken
21. Metal covering an opening in a floppy disk's plastic shell
25. The size of a storage device
26. Usually consists of several inflexible, circular disks on which data is stored electronically
27. Collection of removable hard disks

Down

2. One of the first storage media used with mainframe computers
3. Occurs when a read/write head touches the surface of a hard disk platter
5. Flat, round, portable metal storage medium, usually 4.75 inches in diameter
6. Stores images of documents on sheet film
7. Silver-colored compact disc that can contain text, graphics, video, and sound
9. Holds items such as data, instructions, and information for future use
10. Process of preparing a disk for reading and writing by organizing the disk into storage locations
12. Process of transferring items from a storage medium into memory
13. Stores images of documents on roll film
14. Simplest RAID storage design with one backup disk for each disk
16. Consists of two to eight sectors
19. Process of transferring items from memory to a storage medium
20. Thin, credit card-sized device that fits into a personal computer expansion slot
21. Controller that can support multiple disk drives, as well as other peripherals
22. The most widely used controller, or interface, for hard disks
23. Duplicate of a file, program, or disk that can be used if the original is lost
24. Table of information used to locate files on a disk

Self Test Answers

Matching

1. *c* [p. 6.4]
2. *f* [p. 6.10]
3. *i* [p. 6.15]
4. *l* [p. 6.19]
5. *a* [p. 6.22]
6. *d* [p. 6.23]
7. *g* [p. 6.24]
8. *e* [p. 6.25]
9. *j* [p. 6.26]
0. *b* [p. 6.26]

True/False

1. *T* [p. 6.2]
2. *T* [p. 6.5]
3. *F* [p. 6.6]
4. *F* [p. 6.7]
5. *T* [p. 6.10]
6. *F* [p. 6.11]
7. *T* [p. 6.16]
8. *F* [p. 6.19]
9. *T* [p. 6.23]
0. *T* [p. 6.24]

Multiple Choice

1. *b* [p. 6.3]
2. *c* [p. 6.5]
3. *a* [p. 6.7]
4. *d* [p. 6.9]
5. *d* [p. 6.13]
6. *d* [p. 6.14]
7. *b* [p. 6.16]
8. *a* [p. 6.19]
9. *b* [p. 6.21]
0. *d* [p. 6.27]

Fill in the Blanks

1. *disk* [p. 6.2]
2. *Formatting* [p. 6.5]
3. *write-protect notch* [p. 6.6]
4. *backup* [p. 6.9]
5. *head crash* [p. 6.13]
6. *ATA* or *AT Attachment* [p. 6.14]
7. *jewel box* [p. 6.18]
8. *compact disc read-only memory* [p. 6.19]
9. *Type III cards* [p. 6.25]
0. *computer output microfilm (COM) recorder* [p. 6.26]

Complete the Table

3.5-INCH FLOPPY DISK DENSITIES

	Double Density (DD)	**High Density (HD)**
Capacity	*720 KB*	*1.44 MB*
Number of sides	2	2
Number of tracks	80	*80*
Sectors per track	*9*	*18*
Bytes per sector	*512*	512
Sectors per disk	*1,440*	*2,880*

Things to Think About

Answers will vary.

Puzzle Answer

Storage

	1 D	V	D	R	O	2 M											3 H		
						4 A	C	5 C	E	S	S	T	I	6 M	E		E		7 C
						G		D						I		8 R	A	I	D
9 S	T	R	I	P	I	N	G		10 F		11 T	12 R	A	C	K		D		R
T						E			O			E		R			C		O
O		13 M				T			R			A		O			R		M
R		I		14 M		I			M			D		F			A		
A		C		I		C		15 P	A	R	T	I	T	I	O	N	S		16 C
G		R		R		T			T			N		C			H		L
E		O		R		A			T			G		H					U
		17 F	L	O	P	P	Y	D	I	S	K		18 S	E	C	T	O	R	S
		I		R		E			N										T
		L		I					G										E
		M		N		19 W					20 P		21 S	H	U	T	T	22 E	R
				G		R		23 B			C		C					I	
						I		A			C		S					D	
		24 F				T		25 C	A	P	A	C	I	T	Y			E	
	26 H	A	R	D	D	I	S	K			R								
		T				N		U			27 D	I	S	K	P	A	C	K	
						G		P											

DISCOVERING COMPUTERS 2000

STUDY GUIDE

CHAPTER 7

The Internet

Chapter Overview

This chapter introduces one of the most significant innovations of the past half century – the Internet. The Internet is defined, and the history of the Internet is detailed. You discover how the Internet works and learn about Internet service providers and online services, connecting to the Internet, how data travels the Internet, and Internet addresses. The World Wide Web, search engines, and multimedia on the Web are explained. You become familiar with webcasting, electronic commerce, Web publishing, and other Internet services including e-mail, FTP, Telnet, newsgroups, mailing lists, chat rooms, and portals. Finally, netiquette, cookies, Internet security, and network computers are described.

Chapter Objectives

After completing this chapter, you should be able to:

- Describe how the Internet works
- Recognize how graphics, animation, audio, video, and virtual reality are used on the World Wide Web
- Identify the tools required for Web publishing
- Describe the uses of electronic commerce (e-commerce)
- Explain how e-mail, FTP, Telnet, newsgroups, mailing lists, and chat rooms work
- Identify the rules of netiquette
- Understand security precautions for the Internet
- Explain how network computers are used

Chapter Outline

I. The Internet [p. 7.2]

A network is ____

____

The Internet (or the Net) is ____

____

____

More than 100 million people use the Internet to ______________________________

____

____

II. History of the Internet [p. 7.4]

In 1969, a network called ARPANET, developed by the Advanced Research Projects Agency, became functional, linking scientific and academic researchers in the United States.

In 1986, the National Science Foundation connected its network, called NSFnet, to ARPANET, a configuration that became known as the Internet. NSFnet served as a major backbone. A backbone is ______________________________

____

Today, a variety of corporations, firms, and companies run backbone networks. Even as it grows, the Internet remains ______________________________

____

III. How the Internet works [p. 7.6]

A. Internet service providers and online services [p. 7.6]

An Internet service provider (ISP) is ______________________________

____

Types of ISPs:

- A local ISP ______________________________

  ____

- A national ISP ______________________________

  ____

An online service provides ______________________________

____

B. Connecting to the Internet [p. 7.7]

Many personal computers connect to a local area network (LAN) using a network interface card (NIC). The LAN is connected to an ISP through a leased, high-speed telephone line.

With dial-up access ______________________________

____

C. How data travels the Internet [p. 7.7]

Computers connected to the Internet transfer information using servers and clients.

- A server is ____

  ____
- A client is ____

  ____

Data sent over the Internet is divided into small pieces, called packets, that contain the data, recipient, origin, and reassembling instructions.

Routers are devices that ____

Packet switching is the technique of ____

____

A communications protocol specifies ____

____

The protocol used on the Internet is ____

The Internet communications lines that carry the heaviest traffic are referred to collectively as the Internet backbone.

National ISPs, sometimes called backbone providers, use ______________________

____

D. Internet addresses [p. 7.8]

An IP (Internet protocol) address is ____

____

A domain name is ____

Every domain name contains a top-level domain (TLD) abbreviation that ____

____

Domain name system servers (DNS servers) are Internet computers that store a register of domain names.

IV. The World Wide Web [p. 7.10]

The World Wide Web (WWW), or Web, consists of ______________________

____

Links allow users to ____

____

A Web page is ____

A Web site is ____

A URL (Uniform Resource Locator) is ____

____

Most Web page URLs begin with http://, which stands for hypertext transfer protocol, the communications protocol used to transfer Web pages.

A Web server is ______________________________

A Webmaster is ______________________________

A. Search engines [p. 7.12]

A search engine is a software program that ______________________________

____

B. Multimedia on the Web [p. 7.12]

Most browsers can display multimedia elements on a Web page. Sometimes, however, a browser might need an additional program.

- A plug-in ______________________________
- A helper application ______________________________

Java is ______________________________

Applets are ______________________________

1. Graphics [p. 7.12]

Graphics ______________________________

____

Common file formats for graphical images on the Web:

- A JPEG (Joint Photographic Experts Group) file ______________________________

  ____

- A GIF (Graphics Interchange Format) file ______________________________

  ____

A thumbnail is ______________________________

2. Animation [p. 7.14]

Animation is ______________________________

____

An animated GIF ______________________________

____

3. Audio [p. 7.16]

Simple Web audio applications consist of ______________________________

____

Streaming audio enables ______________________________

____

RealAudio is ______________________________

____

Internet telephone service enables ______________________________

____

4. Video [p. 7.17]
   Simple Web video applications consist of ______________________________

   ____

   Streaming video allows ____

   ____

   RealVideo is ____

   ____

   The Motion Picture Experts Group (MPEG) defines a popular video compression standard.
5. Virtual reality [p. 7.18]
   Virtual reality (VR) is ____

   ____

   Virtual reality modeling language (VRML) is __________________________

   ____

V. Webcasting [p. 7.18]

Browsers once supported only pull technology, in which information is requested, or pulled, from a Web site by entering a URL or clicking a link.

Today's browsers also support push technology, in which ____________________

____

A channel is ____

____

Webcasting is the concept of using ___________________________________

____

VI. Electronic commerce [p. 7.19]

Electronic commerce (e-commerce) is conducting ________________________

____

Electronic data interchange (EDI) is ____________________________________

____

Electronic money (e-moncy) or digital cash is ___________________________

____

- A digital certificate is ____

  ____

- Electronic credit is ____

  ____

VII. Web publishing [p. 7.20]

Personal Web pages are ______________________

Hypertext markup language (HTML) is ______________________

____

Tags are ______________________

Web publishing ______________________

____

Web hosting services provide ______________________

A submission service is ______________________

____

VIII. Other Internet services [p. 7.24]

A. E-mail [p. 7.24]

E-mail (electronic mail) is ______________________

____

Using an e-mail program, messages can be created, sent, received, forwarded, stored, printed, and deleted.

An e-mail address is ______________________

A mail server is ______________________

____

Most e-mail software includes encoding schemes that ______________________

____

B. FTP [p. 7.26]

FTP (file transfer protocol) is ______________________

____

An FTP server is ______________________

____

An FTP site is ______________________

____

An FTP program is used to ______________________

C. Telnet [p. 7.27]

Telnet is ______________________

____

D. Newsgroups [p. 7.27]

A newsgroup is ______________________

____

A news server is ____________________

A newsreader is a program used to access a newsgroup.

An article is ____________________

Posting is the process of ____________________

A thread is ____________________

E. Mailing lists [p. 7.28]

A mailing list is ____________________

____

When you subscribe to a mailing list, you add your name and e-mail address to it; when you unsubscribe, you remove your name.

F. Chat rooms [p. 7.29]

A chat is ____________________

____

A chat room refers to ____________________

____

G. Portals [p. 7.29]

A portal is ____________________

____

IX. Netiquette [p. 7.30]

Netiquette is ____________________

____

Rules of Netiquette: ____________________

____

____

____

____

X. Using the Internet: cookies and security [p. 7.30]

A. Cookies [p. 7.31]

A cookie is ____________________

____

Cookies are used to ____________________

____

B. Internet security [p. 7.32]

Filtering software allows ____________________

____

Confidentiality on the Internet can be enhanced by ______________________

____

XI. Network computers [p. 7.33]

A network computer (NC) is ____

____

- A network personal computer (NetPC) is______________________________

  ____

- A set-top box is____

  ____

Self Test

Matching

1. ____ Web browser
2. ____ search engine
3. ____ plug-in
4. ____ helper application
5. ____ Internet telephone software
6. ____ e-mail program
7. ____ FTP program
8. ____ Telnet
9. ____ newsreader
10. ____ filtering software

a. a software program used to upload files from your computer to an FTP site

b. a software program used to access and view Web pages

c. a software program, included with most browsers, used to participate in a newsgroup

d. a software program that runs multimedia elements within the browser window

e. a software program used to compose and store multiple Web pages

f. a software program that can digitize, compress, and transmit conversations

g. a software program used to create, send, receive, forward, store, and print messages

h. a software program that stores personal data on a client computer

i. a software program that runs multimedia elements in a separate window

j. a software program that allows parents to block access to certain material on the Internet

k. a software program that helps locate Web sites, Web pages, and Internet files

l. a software program that enables you to connect to a remote computer on the Internet

True/False

____ 1. Although each network that constitutes the Internet is owned by a public or private organization, no single organization owns or controls the Internet.

____ 2. Because of their size, national ISPs offer fewer services and generally have a smaller technical support staff than local ISPs.

____ 3. In general, the first portion of each IP (Internet protocol) address identifies the specific computer, and the last portion identifies the network.

____ 4. Although multimedia Web pages often require more time to download because they contain large files such as video or audio clips, the pages usually are worth the wait.

____ 5. Two of the common formats used for audio files on the Internet are JPEG and GIF.

____ 6. Just like paper money, digital cash is reusable and anonymous; that is, the vendor has no information about the buyer.

____ 7. To develop a Web page, you have to be a computer programmer or learn advanced HTML.

____ 8. When you receive an e-mail message, it is placed in your mail box, which is a storage location on the computer that connects you to the Internet.

____ 9. Few FTP sites allow anonymous FTP, whereby anyone can transfer some files.

____ 10. Some mailing lists are called LISTSERVs, named after a popular list software product.

Multiple Choice

____ 1. What is the bulk of communications activity on the Internet called?
   a. discourse
   b. business
   c. movement
   d. traffic

____ 2. In the URL http://www.sportsline.com/mlb/index.html, what is http://?
   a. the protocol
   b. the domain name
   c. the path
   d. the document name

____ 3. For what type of images does the GIF format work best?
   a. scanned photographs
   b. line drawings and simple cartoons
   c. multi-hued artwork
   d. images with smooth color variations

____ 4. What process transfers audio and video data in a continuous and even flow, allowing users to access a file before it has been transmitted completely?
   a. subscribing
   b. routing
   c. streaming
   d. browsing

____ 5. Typically, video files compressed with the standard defined by the Motion Picture Experts Group have what file extension?
   a. .mpg
   b. .peg
   c. .meg
   d. .mpe

____ 6. What is a channel?
a. a small piece into which data sent over the Internet is divided
b. a preselected Web site that automatically can send updated information
c. a high-speed network that connects regional and local networks
d. the fastest available path to a recipient's computer

____ 7. What companies provide storage for Web pages at a reasonable monthly fee?
a. Web page wizards
b. Web page publishers
c. Web browser facilitators
d. Web hosting services

____ 8. What communications protocol is used to retrieve e-mail from a server?
a. SMTP (Simple Mail Transfer Protocol)
b. POP (Post Office Protocol)
c. HTTP (Hypertext Transfer Protocol)
d. ISP (Internet Service Protocol)

____ 9. Which of the following is *not* a rule of netiquette?
a. keep messages brief, using proper grammar and spelling
b. read the FAQ (frequently asked questions), if one exists
c. assume all material is accurate and up to date
d. be careful when using sarcasm and humor

____ 10. Why do Web sites use cookies?
a. to track user preferences
b. to ascertain how regularly a site is visited
c. to target advertisements
d. all of the above

Fill in the Blanks

1. In a network, a(n) ____________________ is any computer directly connected to the network.
2. A(n) ____________________ is a local telephone number provided by an ISP for Internet access.
3. Most Web sites have a starting point, called a(n) ____________________, which provides information about the site's purpose and content.
4. Similar to an applet, a(n) ____________________ is a small program that can be downloaded and run in a browser, adding multimedia capabilities to Web pages.
5. The ____________________ format, which is a patent-free replacement for the GIF, is a compressed file format that supports multiple colors and resolutions.
6. A(n) ____________________ is text that is animated to scroll across the screen, serving as a ticker to display stock updates, news, sports scores, or weather.
7. Using VRML, a developer can create a(n) ____________________, which is an entire 3-D site that contains infinite space and depth.

8. With push technology, Web content can be viewed whether you are online or ____________________ – that is, when you are not connected to the Internet.
9. With electronic credit, a small program, called a(n)____________________ stores your address and credit card information on your computer's hard disk.
10. The entire collection of Internet newsgroups is called ____________________, which contains thousands of newsgroups on a multitude of topics.

Complete the Table

TOP-LEVEL DOMAIN ABBREVIATIONS

Top-Level Domain Abbreviations	Type of Organization
______	Commercial organizations, businesses, and companies
edu	____________________
______	Government institutions
org	____________________
______	Arts and cultural-oriented entities
info	____________________
______	Recreation/entertainment sources
web	____________________

Things to Think About

1. How is an ISP similar to, and different from, an online service? Which would you use to access the Internet? Why?
2. Compared to conventional commerce, what are the advantages, and disadvantages, of e-commerce? For what products is e-commerce most, and least, suited? Why?
3. Why is a moderated newsgroup considered more valuable than a newsgroup that is not moderated? What topics might be dealt with more effectively in a newsgroup that is not moderated? Why?
4. What netiquette rules or guidelines do you think are most important? What rules are least important? Why?

Puzzle

Write the word described by each clue in the puzzle below. Words can be written forward or backward, across, up and down, or diagonally. The initial letter of each word already appears in the puzzle.

S	T										F
P						S					
	G							S			
	S				C						T
	U						J				H
		R	E								
			L								
L									B	A	
			A								H
									A		
			M								
											T

Pentagon agency whose networking project formed the roots of the Internet

any computer directly connected to a network

communications activity on the Internet

a computer that manages the resources on a network and provides a centralized storage area

small pieces into which data sent over the Internet is divided

devices that send packets along the fastest available path

allow users to navigate quickly from one Web document to another

unique address of a Web page

software program used to access and view Web pages

first media used to enhance the text-based Internet

programming language designed for use on the Internet

small programs that can be downloaded and run in a browser window

small version of a larger graphical image; click it to display the full-sized image

animated text that scrolls across the screen

common format used for audio files on the Internet

the process of transferring data in a continuous and even flow

HTML codes that specify how Web page elements display and where links lead

ASCII file extension in which HTML documents must be saved to display as a Web page

copy a Web page from your computer to the Web server

previously entered newsgroup article

save a newsgroup location in your newsreader so it is accessed easily

mailing lists named after a popular mailing list software product

real-time typed conversation that takes place on a computer

unsolicited e-mail message or newsgroup posting

symbols used to express emotions (like :) for smile)

message that reveals a game solution or movie ending

frequently asked questions

Self Test Answers

Matching

1. *b* [p. 7.11]
2. *k* [p. 7.12]
3. *d* [p. 7.12]
4. *i* [p. 7.12]
5. *f* [p. 7.16]
6. *g* [p. 7.24]
7. *a* [p. 7.26]
8. *l* [p. 7.27]
9. *c* [p. 7.27]
0. *j* [p. 7.32]

True/False

1. *T* [p. 7.2]
2. *F* [p. 7.6]
3. *F* [p. 7.8]
4. *T* [p. 7.12]
5. *F* [p. 7.16]
6. *T* [p. 7.20]
7. *F* [p. 7.20]
8. *T* [p. 7.24]
9. *F* [p. 7.26]
0. *T* [p. 7.28]

Multiple Choice

1. *d* [p. 7.5]
2. *a* [p. 7.11]
3. *b* [p. 7.14]
4. *c* [p. 7.16]
5. *a* [p. 7.17]
6. *b* [p. 7.19]
7. *d* [p. 7.23]
8. *b* [p. 7.25]
9. *c* [p. 7.30]
0. *d* [p. 7.31]

Fill in the Blanks

1. *host node* or *host* [p. 7.4]
2. *point of presence (POP)* [p. 7.6]
3. *home page* [p. 7.10]
4. *ActiveX control* [p. 7.12]
5. *PNG (portable network graphics)* [p. 7.14]
6. *marquee* [p. 7.14]
7. *VR world* [p. 7.18]
8. *offline* [p. 7.19]
9. *wallet* [p. 7.20]
0. *Usenet* [p. 7.27]

Complete the Table

TOP-LEVEL DOMAIN ABBREVIATIONS

Top-Level Domain Abbreviations	Type of Organization
com	Commercial organizations, businesses, and companies
edu	*Educational institutions*
gov	Government institutions
org	*Non-profit organizations*
arts	Arts and cultural-oriented entities
info	*Information services*
rec	Recreation/entertainment sources
web	*Parties emphasizing Web activities*

Things to Think About

Answers will vary.

Puzzle Answer

S	**T**	R	E	A	M	I	N	G	Q	A	**F**
P	A	C	K	E	T	**S**	E	R	V	E	R
O	**G**	R	A	P	H	I	C	**S**	P	A	M
I	**S**	T	A	H	**C**	I	F	F	A	R	**T**
L	**U**	P	L	O	A	D	**J**	A	V	A	**H**
E	B	**R**	**E**	M	O	T	I	C	O	N	S
R	S	O	**L**	I	S	T	S	E	R	V	S
L	C	U	R	E	S	W	O	R	**B**	**A**	U
I	R	T	**A**	P	P	L	E	T	S	R	**H**
N	I	E	E	L	C	I	T	R	**A**	P	O
K	B	R	**M**	A	R	Q	U	E	E	A	S
S	E	S	L	I	A	N	B	M	U	H	**T**

DISCOVERING COMPUTERS 2000

STUDY GUIDE

CHAPTER 8

Operating Systems and Utility Programs

Chapter Overview

System software is an essential part of a computer system. This chapter defines system software and discusses two types of system software: operating systems and utility programs. You learn what an operating system is and explore user interfaces, operating systems features, and operating system functions. A variety of popular operating systems are described including DOS, Windows 3.x, Windows 95, Windows 98, Windows 2000, Windows CE, the Mac OS, OS/2, UNIX, Linux, and NetWare. You discover what happens when you start a computer and why a boot disk is important. Finally, a number of utility programs are explained.

Chapter Objectives

After completing this chapter, you should be able to:

- Identify the various types of system software
- Differentiate between an operating system and utility program
- Describe the features of operating systems
- Describe the functions of an operating system
- Identify and briefly describe popular operating systems used today
- Explain the startup process for a personal computer
- Discuss the purpose of the following utilities: viewer, file-compression, diagnostic, disk scanner, defragmenter, uninstaller, backup, antivirus, and screen saver

Chapter Outline

I. System software [p. 8.2]

System software consists of ______________________________

____

II. Operating systems [p. 8.2]

An operating system (OS) is ______________________________

____

The operating system sometimes is called the software platform.

Cross-platform applications run ______________________________________

____

The kernel, or core, of an operating system is responsible for ______________

____

____

A memory-resident program, such as the operating system, remains __________

____

A. User interfaces [p. 8.3]

A user interface is ______________________________________

____

Types of user interfaces:

- With a command-line interface, you ______________________________

  ____

  A command language is ______________________________________
- With a graphical user interface, you ______________________________

  ____

  A menu displays ______________________________________

  An icon is ______________________________________

  Graphical user interfaces are described as user-friendly, because ________

  ____

B. Features of operating systems [p. 8.4]

Capabilities of operating systems:

- A single user (or single tasking) operating system allows ____________

  ____
- A multitasking operating system allows ______________________________

  ____
- A multiuser operating system enables ______________________________

  ____
- A multiprocessing operating system can ______________________________

  ____

C. Functions of an operating system [p. 8.6]

1. Memory management [p. 8.6]

   The purpose of memory management is ______________________________

   ____

   A buffer is ______________________________________

   ____

With virtual memory (VM), the operating system ____________________

____

Paging is the technique of ______________________________________

____

Thrashing occurs when an operating system ________________________

____

2. Spooling print jobs [p. 8.7]
   A print job is ____
   With spooling, print jobs are _________________________________

   ____

3. Configuring devices [p. 8.7]
   A device driver is ____

   ____

   Plug and Play is ____

   ____

   An interrupt request (IRQ) is _________________________________

   ____

4. Monitoring system performance [p. 8.9]
   A performance monitor is _____________________________________

   ____

5. Administering security [p. 8.10]
   Log on is the process of _____________________________________

   ____

   - A user name, or user ID, is _________________________________

     ____

   - A password is ____

     ____

6. Managing storage media and files [p. 8.10]
   A file manager performs _____________________________________

   ____

III. Popular operating systems [p. 8.10]

Although early operating systems were device dependent, the trend today is towards device-independent operating systems.

Device dependent operating systems were developed ____________________

____

Proprietary software is ____

____

Device-independent operating systems will run ______________________________

____

- A downward-compatible operating system is ______________________________

  ____

- Upward compatible application software was ______________________________

  ____

A. DOS [p. 8.11]

DOS (Disk Operating System) refers to ______________________________

____

Developed by Microsoft Corporation, DOS used a command-line interface. At one time, DOS was a widely used operating system.

B. Windows 3.x [p. 8.12]

Windows 3.x refers to ____

____

Developed by Microsoft to meet the demand for a graphical user interface, Windows 3.x actually is an operating environment, not an operating system. An operating environment is ______________________________

____

C. Windows 95 [p. 8.12]

Microsoft's Windows 95 (Win95) is ______________________________

____

Advantages of Windows 95: ____

____

____

____

D. Windows 98 [p. 8.12]

Microsoft's Windows 98 (Win98) is ______________________________

____

Advantages of Windows 98: ____

____

____

____

E. Windows 2000 [p. 8.12]

Windows NT was ______________________________

Windows 2000 is ______________________________

____

Features of Windows 2000: ______________________________

____

____

____

F. Windows CE [p. 8.14]

Windows CE is ______________________________

____

G. Mac OS [p. 8.14]

Apple's Macintosh operating system (Mac OS) was ______________________________

____

H. OS/2 [p. 8.14]

OS/2 is ______________________________

____

Features of OS/2 Warp: ______________________________

____

____

I. UNIX [p. 8.16]

UNIX is ______________________________

____

J. Linux [p. 8.16]

Linux is ______________________________

____

K. NetWare [p. 8.17]

Novell's NetWare is ______________________________

____

IV. Starting a computer [p. 8.17]

Booting is the process of ______________________________

____

- A cold boot is when ______________________________
- A warm boot is ______________________________

Steps that occur during a cold boot using the Windows operating system:

1. ______________________________

2. ______________________________

3. ______________________________

4. ______________________________

5. ______________________________

6. ______________________________

7. ______________________________

A. Boot disk [p. 8.20]

A boot disk is ______________________________

V. Utility programs [p. 8.21]

A utility program (utility) is ______________________________

Popular utility programs:

- A file viewer ______________________________
- A file compression utility ______________________________
- A diagnostic utility ______________________________
- A disk scanner ______________________________
- A disk defragmenter ______________________________
- An uninstaller ______________________________

- A backup utility ____

  ____
- An antivirus program ____

  ____
- A screen saver ____

  ____

Self Test

Matching

1. ____ file viewer
2. ____ file compression
3. ____ diagnostic
4. ____ disk scanner
5. ____ disk defragmenter
6. ____ uninstaller
7. ____ backup
8. ____ restore program
9. ____ antivirus program
10. ____ screen saver

a. utility part that reverses the backup process and returns files to their original form
b. utility that permanently etches images on a monitor screen
c. utility that prevents, detects, and removes viruses from memory or storage devices
d. utility that reduces the size of a file so it takes up less storage space
e. utility that detects and corrects disk problems and searches for and removes unwanted files
f. utility that causes the screen to display a moving image after a period of inactivity
g. utility, such as Quick View or Imaging Preview, that displays the contents of a file
h. utility that compiles technical information about a computer's hardware
i. utility that copies selected files, or the entire hard disk, onto another disk or tape
j. utility that removes an application, as well as any associated entries in the system files
k. utility that contains and loads system configuration information
l. utility that reorganizes files and unused space on a computer's hard disk

True/False

____ 1. With a multitasking operating system, the application you currently are working on is in the background, and the others that are running but not being used are in the foreground.

____ 2. To stop thrashing, you should quit the application that stopped responding.

____ 3. With spooling, multiple print jobs are queued, or lined up, in the buffer.

____ 4. If you add a new device to your computer, such as a printer, its driver must be installed before the device will be operational.

____ 5. The disadvantage of device-independent operating systems is that if you change computer models or vendors, you cannot retain existing application software files and data files.

____ 6. Today, DOS is widely used because it offers a graphical user interface and can take full advantage of modern 32-bit microprocessors.

____ 7. Although designed for use on smaller computing devices, Windows CE requires a great deal of memory.

____ 8. When using Windows, you typically can perform a warm boot, also called a warm start, by pressing a combination of keyboard keys (CTRL+ALT+DEL), selecting options from a menu, or pressing the Reset button.

____ 9. During the boot process, if an operating system disk is not inserted into drive A, the BIOS looks in drive C, which is the designation usually given to the first hard disk.

____ 10. When the contents of a file are gathered across two or more contiguous sectors on a disk, the file is fragmented.

Multiple Choice

____ 1. Today, most operating systems support what capabilities?
  a. single tasking and multiuser
  b. multitasking and multiuser
  c. multiuser and multiprocessing
  d. multiprocessing and single tasking

____ 2. Buffers, swap files, pages, paging, and thrashing all are terms related to what basic function of an operating system?
  a. memory management
  b. configuring devices
  c. monitoring system performance
  d. administering security

____ 3. What is the program that manages and intercepts print jobs and places them in the queue called?
  a. the print driver
  b. the print spooler
  c. the print buffer
  d. the print saver

____ 4. Which of the following was *not* an operating system, but instead was an operating environment for DOS?
  a. Windows 3.x
  b. Windows 95
  c. Windows 98
  d. Windows NT

____ 5. What popular Web browser was included with Windows 98?
  a. Windows Explorer
  b. Windows CE
  c. Microsoft Internet Explorer
  d. Microsoft Auto PC

____ 6. What operating system was proprietary; that is, limited to a specific computer model?
   a. Linux
   b. UNIX
   c. Windows 98
   d. Mac OS

____ 7. What is a weakness of UNIX?
   a. it is a single user, single tasking operating system, and no versions are available for most computers
   b. it is incapable of handling a high volume of transactions or working with multiple CPUs using multiprocessing
   c. it has a command-line interface, and many of its commands are difficult to remember and use
   d. all of the above

____ 8. What is the drive from which your computer starts (usually drive C – the hard disk) called?
   a. the start drive
   b. the registry drive
   c. the boot drive
   d. the BIOS drive

____ 9. Disk Cleanup is an example of what type of utility?
   a. a disk scanner
   b. a diagnostic utility
   c. a disk defragmenter
   d. a file compression utility

____ 10. A restore program generally is included with what type of utility?
   a. screen saver
   b. antivirus
   c. uninstaller
   d. backup

Fill in the Blanks

1. A computer with separate CPUs can serve as a(n) ____________________; that is, one that continues to operate even if one of its components fails.
2. A(n) ____________________ is the area of the hard disk used for virtual memory.
3. In virtual memory, a(n) ____________________ is the amount of data and program instructions exchanged at a given time.
4. The ____________________ is firmware that contains a computer's startup instructions.
5. The BIOS executes a series of tests, called the ____________________, which check the various system components.

6. In Windows, the ___________________ consists of several files that contain the system configuration information.
7. Compressed files, sometimes called ___________________, usually have a .zip extension.
8. The process of ___________________ – that is, reorganizing a disk so files are stored in contiguous sectors – speeds up disk access and thus the performance of the entire computer.
9. A(n) ___________________ is a program that copies itself into other programs and spreads through multiple computers.
10. Screen savers were developed to prevent a problem called ___________________, in which images could be permanently etched on a monitor's screen.

Complete the Table

WINDOWS 98 FEATURES

Feature	Description
_______________	Allows you to set up Windows so icons on the desktop and the file names in Windows Explorer work like Web links.
Increased speed	____
_______________	Makes it possible to use several monitors at the same time to run programs or play games with multiple views.
Tune-Up Wizard	____
_______________	Reviews device drivers, compares findings with a Web database, and then recommends and installs updates.
Universal Serial Bus Support	____
_______________	An improved version of the File Allocation Table that allows hard drives larger than 2 GB to be formatted as a single drive.
Registry Checker	____

Things to Think About

1. How has the concept of user-friendly affected the development of operating systems? What operating systems seem the most, and least, user-friendly? Why?
2. What three functions of an operating system are most important for a home computer user? For an office computer user? Why?

3. Why is a boot disk important? In Windows, how can you create a boot disk?
4. From most important to least important, how would you rank the utility programs described in this chapter? Why did you rank the programs as you did?

Puzzle

The terms described by the phrases below are written below each line in code. Break the code by writing the correct term above the coded word. Then, use your broken code to translate the final sentence.

1. consists of the programs that control the operations of the computer and its devices ________ OUOPAI OKBPSWNA
2. a set of programs containing instructions that coordinate all of the activities among hardware ________ KLANWPEJC OUOPAI
3. the core of an operating system ________ GANJAH
4. the part of the software with which you interact ________ QOAN EJPANBWYA
5. displays a set of available commands or options from which you can choose ________ IAJQ
6. a small image that represents an item such as a program, an instruction, or a file ________ EYKJ
7. operating system capability that allows a user to work on two or more applications that reside in memory ________ IQHPEPWOGEJC
8. allocates a portion of a storage medium to function as additional RAM ________ RENPQWH IAIKNU
9. what happens when an operating system spends too much time paging instead of executing software ________ PDNWODEJC
10. small program that converts commands into instructions a hardware device understands ________ ZNERAN
11. a communications line between a device and the CPU ________ EJPANNQLP NAMQAOP
12. combination of characters associated with a user name that allows access to certain computer resources ________ LWOOSKNZ
13. program that performs functions related to storage and file management ________ BEHA IWJWCAN
14. turning on a computer after it has been powered off completely ________ YKHZ XKKP
15. several files in which the system configuration information is contained ________ NACEOPNU
16. floppy disk that contains certain operating system commands that will start the computer ________ XKKP ZEOG

17. a type of system software that performs a specific task, usually related to managing a computer ____________ QPEHEPU LNKCNWI
18. compressed files, usually with a .zip extension ____________ VELLAZ BEHAO
19. what you do to restore a zipped file to its original form ____________ QJYKILNAOO
20. a program that copies itself onto other programs and spreads through multiple computers ____________ RENQO

____

W JAS LNKCNWI YWHHAZ OUOPAI YKIIWJZAN ZAHQTA IWGAO

____

YDKKOEJC WJ KLANWPEJC OUOPAI AWOEAN XU AHEIEJWPEJC PDA

____

JAAZ PK IWGA W YDKEYA, WHHKSEJC QOANO PK OSEPYD AWOEHU

____

WIKJC QL PK PDENPU-PSK ZEBBANAJP KLANWPEJC OUOPAIO.

Self Test Answers

Matching

1. *g* [p. 8.21]
2. *d* [p. 8.22]
3. *h* [p. 8.22]
4. *e* [p. 8.23]
5. *l* [p. 8.23]
6. *j* [p. 8.24]
7. *i* [p. 8.24]
8. *a* [p. 8.24]
9. *c* [p. 8.25]
0. *f* [p. 8.25]

True/False

1. *F* [p. 8.5]
2. *T* [p. 8.7]
3. *T* [p. 8.7]
4. *T* [p. 8.8]
5. *F* [p. 8.10]
6. *F* [p. 8.11]
7. *F* [p. 8.14]
8. *T* [p. 8.17]
9. *T* [p. 8.19]
0. *F* [p. 8.23]

Multiple Choice

1. *b* [p. 8.4]
2. *a* [p. 8.6]
3. *b* [p. 8.7]
4. *a* [p. 8.12]
5. *c* [p. 8.12]
6. *d* [p. 8.14]
7. *c* [p. 8.16]
8. *c* [p. 8.20]
9. *a* [p. 8.23]
0. *d* [p. 8.24]

Fill in the Blanks

1. *fault-tolerant computer* [p. 8.5]
2. *swap file* [p. 8.6]
3. *page* [p. 8.7]
4. *BIOS (basic input/output system* [p. 8.18]
5. *power-on self test (POST)* [p. 8.19]
6. *registry* [p. 8.19]
7. *zipped files* [p. 8.22]
8. *defragmentation* [p. 8.23]
9. *virus* [p. 8.25]
0. *ghosting* [p. 8.25]

Complete the Table

WINDOWS 98 FEATURES

Feature	Description
Active Desktop™	Allows you to set up Windows so icons on the desktop and the file names in Windows Explorer work like Web links.
Increased speed	*Faster startup and shutdown of Windows. Loads 32-bit applications faster.*
Multiple display support	Makes it possible to use several monitors at the same time to run programs or play games with multiple views.
Tune-Up Wizard	*Makes programs run faster, checks for hard disk problems, and frees up hard disk space.*
Update Wizard	Reviews device drivers, compares findings with a Web database, and then recommends and installs updates.

Feature	Description
Universal Serial Bus Support	*Adds devices to your computer easily without having to restart.*
FAT32	An improved version of the File Allocation Table that allows hard drives larger than 2 GB to be formatted as a single drive.
Registry Checker	*A system maintenance program that finds and fixes registry problems.*

Things to Think About

Answers will vary.

Puzzle Answer

1.	consists of the programs that control the operations of the computer and its devices	*system software* OUOPAI OKBPSWNA
2.	a set of programs containing instructions that coordinate all of the activities among hardware	*operating system* KLANWPEJC OUOPAI
3.	the core of an operating system	*kernel* GANJAH
4.	the part of the software with which you interact	*user interface* QOAN EJPANBWYA
5.	displays a set of available commands or options from which you can choose	*menu* IAJQ
6.	a small image that represents an item such as a program, an instruction, or a file	*icon* EYKJ
7.	operating system capability that allows a user to work on two or more applications that reside in memory	*multitasking* IQHPEPWOGEJC
8.	allocates a portion of a storage medium to function as additional RAM	*virtual memory* RENPQWH IAIKNU
9.	what happens when an operating system spends too much time paging instead of executing software	*thrashing* PDNWODEJC
10.	small program that converts commands into instructions a hardware device understands	*driver* ZNERAN
11.	a communications line between a device and the CPU	*interrupt request* EJPANNQLP NAMQAOP

12.	combination of characters associated with a user name that allows access to certain computer resources	*password* LWOOSKNZ
13.	program that performs functions related to storage and file management	*file manager* BEHA IWJWCAN
14.	turning on a computer after it has been powered off completely	*cold boot* YKHZ XKKP
15.	several files in which the system configuration information is contained	*registry* NACEOPNU
16.	floppy disk that contains certain operating system commands that will start the computer	*boot disk* XKKP ZEOG
17.	a type of system software that performs a specific task, usually related to managing a computer	*utility program* QPEHEPU LNKCNWI
18.	compressed files, usually with a .zip extension	*zipped files* VELLAZ BEHAO
19.	what you do to restore a zipped file to its original form	*uncompress* QJYKILNAOO
20.	a program that copies itself onto other programs and spreads through multiple computers	*virus* RENQO

A new program called System Commander Deluxe makes
W JAS LNKCNWI YWHHAZ OUOPAI YKIIWJZAN ZAHQTA IWGAO

choosing an operating system easier by eliminating the
YDKKOEJC WJ KLANWPEJC OUOPAI AWOEAN XU AHEIEJWPEJC PDA

need to make a choice, allowing users to switch easily
JAAZ PK IWGA W YDKEYA, WHHKSEJC QOANO PK OSEPYD AWOEHU

among up to thirty-two different operating systems.
WIKJC QL PK PDENPU-PSK ZEBBANAJP KLANWPEJC OUOPAIO.

DISCOVERING COMPUTERS 2000

STUDY GUIDE

CHAPTER 9

Communications and Networks

Chapter Overview

This chapter explores communications and networks. Communications is defined and the uses of communications are detailed, including e-mail, voice mail, fax, telecommuting, videoconferencing, groupware, global positioning systems, bulletin board systems, and the Internet. You learn what a communications channel is and compare physical transmission media and wireless transmission media. Transmission characteristics, including signal type, transmission modes, transmission direction, and transfer rates are described. You become acquainted with the telephone network and the difference between dial-up lines and dedicated lines. A communications channel example is presented, communications software is characterized, and communications devices (modems, cable modems, multiplexers, network interface cards, and network connections) are discussed. Finally, you investigate networks and topics such as local area networks, network operating systems, types of LANs, wide area networks, metropolitan area networks, network topologies, communications protocols, and intranets.

Chapter Objectives

After completing this chapter, you should be able to:

- Define the components required for successful communications
- Describe uses of communications
- Identify the various types of transmission media
- Explain the purpose of communications software
- Describe commonly used communications devices
- Explain the difference between a local area network and a wide area network
- Understand the various communications protocols
- Identify uses of intranets and extranets

Chapter Outline

I. Communications [p. 9.2]

Communications (data communications or telecommunications) describes ______

____

The basic model for communications consists of:

- ____________________
- ____________________
- ____________________
- ____________________
- ____________________
- communications software

II. Uses of communications [p. 9.3]

A. E-mail [p. 9.3]

E-mail (electronic mail) is ____________________

____

B. Voice mail [p. 9.3]

Voice mail allows ____________________

____

C. Fax [p. 9.3]

A fax (facsimile) machine is ____________________

____

D. Telecommuting [p. 9.4]

Telecommuting is ____________________

____

E. Videoconferencing [p. 9.4]

Videoconferencing involves ____________________

____

F. Groupware [p. 9.5]

Groupware is ____________________

____

G. Global positioning system [p. 9.5]

A global positioning system consists of ____________________

____

H. Bulletin board system [p. 9.5]

An electronic bulletin board system (BBS) is ____________________

____

I. The Internet [p. 9.6]

The Internet is ____________________

____

1. The Web [p. 9.6]

   The Web consists of ____________________

   ____

2. E-commerce [p. 9.6]
   E-commerce includes ______________________________

   ____

3. Telephony [p. 9.6]
   Internet telephony enables ______________________________

   ____

III. Communications channel [p. 9.7]

A channel is ______________________________

Transmission media consists of ______________________________

____

- Physical transmission media use ______________________________

  ____

- Wireless transmission media send ______________________________

  ____

IV. Physical transmission media [p. 9.7]

A. Twisted-pair cable [p. 9.7]

Twisted-pair cable consists of ______________________________

____

Twisted-pair wire consists of ______________________________

____

- Shielded twisted-pair (STP) cable has ______________________________

  ____

- Unshielded twisted-pair (UTP) cable ______________________________

  ____

B. Coaxial cable [p. 9.8]

Coaxial cable (coax) consists of ______________________________

____

C. Fiber-optic cable [p. 9.8]

Fiber-optic cable consists of ______________________________

____

Advantages of fiber-optic cable include: ______________________________

____

____

V. Wireless transmission media [p. 9.9]

A. Broadcast radio [p. 9.9]

Broadcast radio is ______________________________

____

B. Cellular radio [p. 9.10]

Cellular radio is ______________________________

____

A cellular telephone is ______________________________

____

C. Microwaves [p. 9.10]

Microwaves are ______________________________

____

D. Communications satellite [p. 9.11]

A communications satellite is ______________________________

____

- An uplink is ______________________________
- A downlink is ______________________________

E. Infrared [p. 9.12]

Infrared is ______________________________

____

VI. Transmission characteristics [p. 9.12]

Transmissions can be characterized by the type of signal, mode of transmission, direction of transmission, and rate of transmission.

A. Signal type: analog or digital [p. 9.12]

- An analog signal consists of ______________________________
- Digital signals are ______________________________

Telephone lines carry analog signals. Computers process data as digital signals. A modem converts between digital signals and analog signals.

B. Transmission modes: asynchronous and synchronous [p. 9.13]

- With asynchronous transmission, ______________________________

  ____

  ____

  A *start bit* marks the beginning of a byte, and a *stop bit* marks the end of the byte.

- Synchronous transmission involves ______________________________

  ____

  ____

  Synchronous transmission requires more expensive equipment but provides greater speed and accuracy than asynchronous transmission.

C. Transmission direction: simplex, half-duplex, and full-duplex [p. 9.14]

The direction in which data flows is classified in one of three types:

- In simplex transmission, data flows ______________________________

  ____

- In half-duplex transmission, data can flow ______________________________

  ____

- In full-duplex transmission, data can flow ______________________________

  ____

D. Transfer rates [p. 9.14]

Transfer rate is ______________________________

Transfer rate is expressed in bits per second (bps).

Bandwidth is ______________________________

____

For analog signals, bandwidth is expressed in hertz (Hz) or cycles per second (cps). For digital signals, bandwidth is expressed in bits per second (bps).

VII. The telephone network [p. 9.15]

The public switched telephone network (PSTN) is ______________________________

____

Data, instructions, and information can be sent over the PSTN using dial-up lines or dedicated lines.

A. Dial-up lines [p. 9.16]

A dial-up line is ______________________________

____

B. Dedicated lines [p. 9.16]

A dedicated line is ______________________________

____

A leased line is ______________________________

____

Popular types of digital leased lines:

1. ISDN lines [p. 9.17]

   Integrated Services Digital Network (ISDN) is ____________________

   ____

   - Basic Rate Interface (BRI) ____________________

2. Digital subscriber lines [p. 9.17]

   A digital subscriber line (DSL) uses ____________________

   ____

   - Asymmetric digital subscriber line (ADSL) is ____________________

     ____

3. T-carrier lines [p. 9.17]

   A T-carrier line is ____________________

   ____

   - A T-1 line can carry ____________________
   - A T-3 line is equal to ____________________

4. Asynchronous transfer mode [p. 9.17]

   Asynchronous transfer mode (ATM) is ____________________

   ____

VIII. Communications channel example [p. 9.18]

When a typical communications channel sends a request over the Internet:

Step 1: A PC's request for information travels to the ISP.

Step 2: ____

____

Step 3: ____

Step 4: ____

IX. Communications software [p. 9.18]

Communications software consists of ____________________

____

Features of communications software:

- The dialing feature allows ____________________

  ____

- File transfer allows ____________________

  ____

- The terminal emulation feature allows ____________________

  ____

- The Internet access feature allows ______________________________

  ____

X. Communications devices [p. 9.20]

A communications device is ______________________________

____

A. Modems [p. 9.20]

A modem converts between ______________________________

____

- An external modem is ______________________________

  ____

- An internal modem is ______________________________

  ____

B. Cable modems [p. 9.21]

A cable modem is ______________________________

____

- An external cable modem is ______________________________

  ____

- An internal cable modem is ______________________________

  ____

C. Multiplexer [p. 9.22]

A multiplexer (MUX) is ______________________________

____

D. Network interface card [p. 9.22]

A network interface card (NIC) is ______________________________

____

E. Connecting networks [p. 9.23]

Devices used to interconnect networks:

1. Hub [p. 9.23]

   A hub is ______________________________

   ____

2. Repeater [p. 9.24]

   A repeater is ______________________________

   ____

3. Bridge [p. 9.24]
   A bridge is______________________________
   ____
4. Gateway [p. 9.24]
   A gateway is ______________________________
   ____
5. Router [p. 9.24]
   A router is ______________________________
   ____

XI. Networks [p. 9.24]

A network is ______________________________

____

Networks promote:

- ______________________
- ______________________
- ______________________
- ______________________

Networks exist in a range of sizes, and can connect computers of all sizes. Two widely used types of networks are local area networks and wide area networks.

A. Local area network (LAN) [p. 9.25]

A local area network (LAN) is ______________________________

____

B. Network operating system [p. 9.26]

A network operating system (NOS) is ______________________________

____

Tasks performed by a NOS:

- ______________________
- ______________________
- ______________________
- ______________________

C. Types of LANs [p. 9.26]

Popular types of LANs are peer-to-peer and client/server. The difference between them is ______________________________

1. Peer-to-peer network [p. 9.26]
   A peer-to-peer network is ______________________________
   ____
   - A peer ______________________________
     ____

2. Client/server network [p. 9.27]

   A client/server network is ____

   ____

   - A server ____

     ____

   - Clients ____

     ____

   A network administrator is ____

   ____

D. Wide area network (WAN) [p. 9.28]

   A wide area network (WAN) is ____

   ____

   Today, a WAN typically consists of two or more LANs connected by routers. The Internet is the world's largest WAN.

E. Metropolitan area network (MAN) [p. 9.29]

   A metropolitan area network (MAN) is ____

   ____

F. Network topologies [p. 9.29]

   The network topology (or network architecture) is ____

   ____

   Commonly used network topologies:

   1. Bus network [p. 9.29]

      A bus network consists of ____

      ____

      The bus is ____

   2. Ring network [p. 9.30]

      A ring network is ____

      ____

   3. Star network [p. 9.30]

      In a star network ____

      ____

      The hub is ____

G. Communications protocols [p. 9.30]

   A protocol is ____

   ____

Widely used protocols:

1. Ethernet [p. 9.30]

   Ethernet is ______________________________

   ____

2. Token ring [p. 9.31]

   A token ring protocol controls ______________________________

   ____

3. TCP/IP [p. 9.32]

   TCP/IP (Transmission control protocol/Internet protocol) is ____________

   ____

H. Intranets [p. 9.32]

Intranets are ______________________________

____

Intranets facilitate working in groups.

Intranet applications and uses include: ______________________________

____

An extranet is ______________________________

____

1. Firewalls [p. 9.33]

   A firewall is ______________________________

   ____

Self Test

Matching

1. ____ e-mail
2. ____ voice mail
3. ____ fax
4. ____ telecommuting
5. ____ videoconferencing
6. ____ groupware
7. ____ global positioning system (GPS)
8. ____ bulletin board system (BBS)
9. ____ the Internet
10. ____ the Web

a. involves using video and computer technology to conduct a meeting between participants
b. a software application that helps groups of people work together on projects
c. employees use communications technology to communicate with an office
d. enables users to talk to other people over the Web
e. includes activities such as shopping, banking, investing, and other uses of electronic money
f. consists of a worldwide collection of electronic documents that have built-in links
g. a document sent and received over telephone lines
h. like an answering machine, allows callers to leave a voice message for the called party
i. a computer that maintains a centralized collection of electronic messages
j. the exchange of text messages and computer files via a communications network
k. a worldwide collection of networks that links millions of users
l. consists of earth-based receivers that analyze satellite signals to determine locations

True/False

____ 1. Once digitized, a voice mail message is stored in a stand-alone fax machine, which is a storage location on a computer in a voice mail system.

____ 2. A voice mailbox scans a printed document, digitizes the text and graphical images, and transmits the digitized data.

____ 3. Electronic data interchange (EDI) is a means of paying for goods and services over the Internet.

____ 4. Microwaves are limited to line-of-sight transmission, which means that microwaves must be transmitted in a straight line with no obstructions.

____ 5. In synchronous transmission, a *start bit* marks the beginning of the byte and a *stop bit* marks the end of the byte.

____ 6. Although a communications channel involves many media and devices, the entire communications process can take less than one second.

____ 7. Cable modems currently can transmit data at speeds of 500 Kbps to 2 Mbps – much faster than either a standard modem or ISDN.

____ 8. To use a bridge, the transmission media used in the LANs have to be the same.

____ 9. The bus topology and the ring topology are used primarily for local area networks.

____ 10. Organizations use firewalls to admit network access to outsiders and to promote employees' access to sensitive data.

Multiple Choice

____ 1. Because you can use the Internet to access many of the same services, usage of what communications technology is declining?
   a. telecommuting
   b. global positioning systems
   c. videoconferencing
   d. bulletin board systems

____ 2. Which of the following is *not* an advantage of fiber-optic cable?
   a. faster data transmission
   b. capability of carrying significantly more signals
   c. less cost than twisted-pair or coaxial cable
   d. better security for signals during transmission

____ 3. With what do cellular radio base stations communicate to send and receive voice and data traffic to and from the public switched telephone network?
   a. a telephone mobile switching office (TMSO)
   b. a mobile switching telephone office (MSTO)
   c. a mobile telephone switching office (MTSO)
   d. a switching telephone mobile office (STMO)

____ 4. What is a VSAT (Very Small Aperture Terminal)?
   a. a small communications satellite used for applications that involve transmitting small amounts of data
   b. an earth-based reflective dish that contains the antenna, transceivers, and equipment for microwave communications
   c. a device that combines two or more input signals into a single stream of data and then transmits it
   d. the central computer that provides a connection point for all devices in a network

____ 5. How is transfer rate usually expressed?
   a. bits per second (bps)
   b. pages per minute (ppm)
   c. cycles per second (cps)
   d. lines per minute (lpm)

____ 6. What is a disadvantage of a dial-up line?
   a. it costs more than making a regular telephone call
   b. computers cannot establish a connection using modems and the PSTN
   c. you cannot control the quality of the connection
   d. all of the above

____ 7. What is the transfer rate of most personal computer modems?
   a. between 14.2 Kbps and 28 Kbps
   b. between 28.8 Kbps and 56 Kbps
   c. between 56.6 Kbps and 112 Kbps
   d. between 112.4 Kbps and 224 Kbps

____ 8. What device sends communications traffic to the appropriate network using the fastest available path?
   a. a repeater
   b. a bridge
   c. a gateway
   d. a router

____ 9. In a client/server network, what type of server, intended for the home user, provides access to the Internet?
   a. a file server
   b. a print server
   c. a database server
   d. a thin server

____ 10. What is one of the major protocols used on the Internet?
   a. Fast Ethernet
   b. TCP/IP
   c. Gigabit Ethernet
   d. token ring

Fill in the Blanks

1. A broad concept called ____________________ includes specific hardware and software that enables members to communicate, manage projects, schedule meetings, and make collaborative decisions.
2. Wires are twisted together to reduce ____________________, which is an electrical disturbance that can degrade communication.
3. Some networks use a(n) ____________________, which both sends and receives signals from wireless devices.
4. The broadcast area for cellular radio is divided into honeycombed-shaped ____________________, each of which covers a specific geographic region.
5. ____________________ orbit at the same rate as the earth, maintaining their positions over the same location of the earth's surface.
6. Telephone service carried by PSTN sometimes is called ____________________.

7. Today, many modems are called ____________________ because they can send and receive computer-prepared documents as faxes.
8. A technique called ____________________ combines multiple signals (analog or digital) for transmission over a single line or media.
9. A(n) ____________________ is a legal agreement issued by software vendors when you purchase a network version of a software package.
10. Ethernet networks use an access method called ____________________ to avoid collisions.

Complete the Table

POPULAR NETWORK OPERATING SYSTEMS

Network Operating System	Operating System Required	LAN type
Novell NetWare	DOS	____________
Artisoft LANtastic	____________	Peer-to-peer
Microsoft Windows 95, Windows 98, and Windows for Workgroups	____________	____________
Microsoft Windows NT	Windows NT	____________
Banyan Vines	____________	Client/server
Microsoft OS/2 LAN Manager	____________	____________

Things to Think About

1. What two communications technologies have had the greatest impact on personal interactions? What technologies have had the greatest impact on business interactions? Why?
2. Why is simplex transmission used for security systems and fire alarms, half-duplex transmission for credit card verification systems and automatic teller machines, and full-duplex transmission for applications with intensive computing requirements?
3. What network capability – hardware sharing, data and information sharing, software sharing, or facilitated communications – would be most important to a school? To a business? To a government office? Why?
4. What network topology – bus, ring, or star – would be best for a school? For a business? For a government office? Why?

Puzzle

All of the words described below appear in the puzzle. Words may be either forward or backward, across, up and down, or diagonal. Circle each word as you find it.

Communications and Networks

```
      P     H T A     A
    G   B   N   A   Q   N
    X     A   V   S     S
      P W   F I O   V J
              D
N A M C O N C E N T R A T O R
G N I T U M M O C E L E T P E
Z G C E P T S C N N M X U R T
H N R N A B E O D I O T P O A
T I O R C U I N E L D R L T E
D R W E K S N F R D E A I O P
I N A T E X T E A E M N N C E
W E V N T A R R R S H E K O R
D K E I S O A E F A U T G L O
N O S L O C N N N E B J E R U
A T L E S N E C I L E T I S T
B E X M U L T I P L E X E R E
C L I E N T S N V S E R V E R
Y Y A W E T A G N E T W O R K
D O W N L I N K T B R I D G E
```

arrangement in which employees work away from the office

involves using video and computer technology to conduct a meeting

worldwide collection of networks that links millions of users

electrical disturbance that can degrade communications

twisted-pair cable with a metal wrapper around each wire

single copper wire surrounded by three layers

communications device that both sends and receives wireless signals

honeycombed-shaped broadcast areas for cellular radio

radio waves that provide high-speed signal transmission

transmission from an earth station to a satellite

transmission from a satellite to an earth station

small communications satellite for transmitting small amounts of data

wireless transmission media that sends signals using light waves

range of frequencies a transmission medium can carry in a period of time

dedicated line rented from a telephone or communications service company

converts between analog and digital signals

device that combines two or more input signals into a single stream

expansion card that enables a device to connect to a network

device that provides a central point for cables in a network

device also called a hub or multistation access unit (MAU)

device that accepts, amplifies, and retransmits a signal

device that connects two LANs using the same protocol

hardware and software that connects networks using different protocols

device that sends communications traffic using the fastest available path

collection of computers and devices connected by communications channels

legal agreement issued with the purchase of the network version of software

network that connects computers in a limited geographical area

computer that controls access to the hardware and software on a network

computers that rely on servers for programs, data, and information

network that covers a large geographical area

backbone network that connects LANs in a city or town

physical cable connecting computers and other devices on a bus network

set of rules and procedures for exchanging information among computers

LAN protocol that allows PCs to contend for network access

protocol that controls network access by requiring a signal to be passed

small pieces into which data sent over the Internet is divided

internal networks that use Internet and Web technologies

intranet that extends to authorized users outside a company

Self Test Answers

Matching

1. *j* [p. 9.3]
2. *h* [p. 9.3]
3. *g* [p. 9.3]
4. *c* [p. 9.4]
5. *a* [p. 9.4]
6. *b* [p. 9.5]
7. *l* [p. 9.5]
8. *i* [p. 9.5]
9. *k* [p. 9.6]
0. *f* [p. 9.6]

True/False

1. *F* [p. 9.3]
2. *F* [p. 9.3]
3. *F* [p. 9.6]
4. *T* [p. 9.11]
5. *F* [p. 9.14]
6. *T* [p. 9.18]
7. *T* [p. 9.21]
8. *F* [p. 9.24]
9. *T* [p. 9.29]
0. *F* [p. 9.33]

Multiple Choice

1. *d* [p. 9.5]
2. *c* [p. 9.8]
3. *c* [p. 9.10]
4. *a* [p. 9.12]
5. *a* [p. 9.14]
6. *c* [p. 9.16]
7. *b* [p. 9.21]
8. *d* [p. 9.24]
9. *d* [p. 9.28]
0. *b* [p. 9.30]

Fill in the Blanks

1. *workgroup computing* [p. 9.5]
2. *noise* [p. 9.7]
3. *transceiver* [p. 9.9]
4. *cells* [p. 9.10]
5. *Geosynchronous satellites* [p. 9.11]
6. *plain old telephone service (POTS)* [p. 9.15]
7. *fax modems* [p. 9.21]
8. *multiplexing* [p. 9.22]
9. *site license* [p. 9.25]
0. *Carrier Sense Multiple Access/Collision Detection (CSMA/CD)* [p. 9.31]

Complete the Table

POPULAR NETWORK OPERATING SYSTEMS

Network Operating System	Operating System Required	LAN type
Novell NetWare	DOS	*Client/server*
Artisoft LANtastic	*DOS*	Peer-to-peer
Microsoft Windows 95, Windows 98, and Windows for Workgroups	*Windows*	*Peer-to-peer*
Microsoft Windows NT	Windows NT	*Client/server*

Network Operating System	Operating System Required	LAN type
Banyan Vines	*UNIX*	Client/server
Microsoft OS/2 LAN Manager	*OS/2*	*Client/server*

Things to Think About

Answers will vary.

Puzzle Answer

Communications and Networks

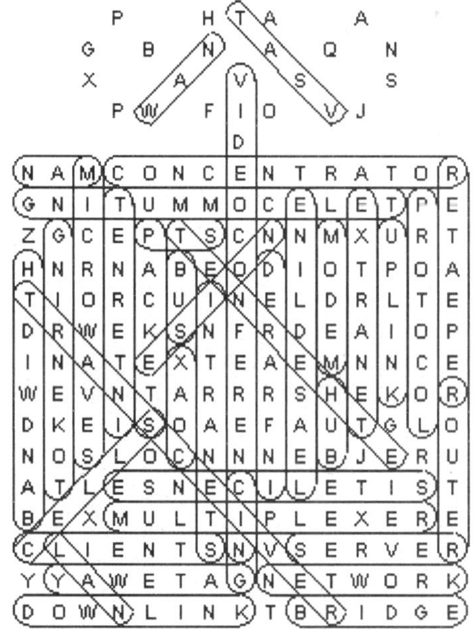

DISCOVERING COMPUTERS 2000

STUDY GUIDE

CHAPTER 10

Databases and Information Management

Chapter Overview

Information is one of an organization's most valuable assets. In this chapter, you examine databases and information management. Data and information are defined and two critically important aspects – data integrity and data security – are considered. The hierarchy of data is presented. You learn the procedures involved in maintaining data, such as adding records, changing records, deleting records, and data validation. File processing systems are contrasted with the database approach. You explore features of database management systems including the data dictionary, data maintenance and retrieval, data security, and backup and recovery. Two popular database models, relational databases and object-oriented databases, are described. Database administration is explained. You study qualities of valuable information, how managers use information, and levels of information users in an organization. Finally, the chapter identifies types of information systems: office information systems, transaction processing systems, management information systems, decision support systems, expert systems, and integrated information systems.

Chapter Objectives

After completing this chapter, you should be able to:

- Explain why data and information are important to an organization
- Identify data maintenance techniques
- Differentiate between file processing and databases
- Discuss the advantages of using a database management system (DBMS)
- Describe the characteristics of relational and object-oriented databases
- Explain how to use a query language
- Discuss the responsibilities of the data and database administrators
- Describe the various types of information systems

Chapter Outline

I. Data and information [p. 10.2]

- Data is ____
- Information is ____

Information is a valuable resource that is difficult, if not impossible, to replace. Because information cannot be generated without data, an organization must manage, maintain, and protect its data.

A database is ____

____

A. Data integrity [p. 10.2]

Data integrity is ____

Garbage in, garbage out (GIGO) is a computing principle that means ________

____

B. Data security [p. 10.3]

Data security involves ____

II. The hierarchy of data [p. 10.3]

Data is organized in a hierarchy in which each higher level consists of one or more elements from the lower level preceding it.

- A character – such as a number, letter, punctuation mark, or other symbol – is represented by a byte (8 bits grouped together in a unit).
- A field is ____

  Fields often are defined by data type and field length.

  The data type specifies ____

  Common data types include:

  - ______________
  - ______________
  - ______________
  - ______________
  - ______________
  - ______________

  The field length is ____
- A record is ____

  A key field is ____
- A data file is ____

  ____
- A database is a group of related data files.

III. Maintaining data [p. 10.4]

Data maintenance refers to ____

A. Adding records [p. 10.5]

Records are added when ____

____

B. Changing records [p. 10.6]

Generally, you change records

(1) ______________________________

(2) ______________________________

C. Deleting records [p. 10.6]

A record is deleted from a file when ______________________________

D. Data validation [p. 10.7]

Validation is ______________________________

____

A validity check ______________________________

Types of validity checks:

1. Alphabetic/numeric check [p. 10.8]

   An alphabetic check ensures ______________________________

   ____

2. Completeness check [p. 10.8]

   A completeness check verifies ______________________________

   ____

3. Range check [p. 10.8]

   A range check determines ______________________________

   ____

4. Consistency check [p. 10.8]

   A consistency check tests ______________________________

   ____

5. Check digit [p. 10.8]

   A check digit verifies ______________________________

   ____

IV. File processing versus databases [p. 10.9]

Almost all application programs use data that is stored in either files or databases.

A. File processing systems [p. 10.9]

In a typical file processing system ______________________________

____

____

Disadvantages of file processing systems:

- Data redundancy ______________________________

  ____

- Isolated data ____

____

B. The database approach [p. 10.10]

With the database approach ____

____

Users access the data in a database using database software, which often is called a database management system (DBMS).

Advantages of the database approach:

- Reduced data redundancy ____

  ____

- Improved data integrity ____

  ____

- Shared data ____

  ____

- Reduced development time ____

  ____

- Easier reporting ____

  ____

Disadvantages of the database approach: ____

____

____

V. Database management systems [p. 10.13]

A database management system (DBMS) is ____

____

Features of a DBMS include a data dictionary and functions such as data maintenance and retrieval, data security, and backup and recovery.

A. Data dictionary [p. 10.14]

A data dictionary stores ____

____

A DBMS uses the data dictionary to perform validation checks and maintain the integrity of data. The data dictionary allows a default value to be specified.

A default value is ____

B. Data maintenance and retrieval [p. 10.14]

A query is a process that involves ____

____

A DBMS provides several methods of accessing data.

- A query language consists of ______________________________

  ____

  Query-by-example (QBE) ______________________________

  ____

- A form is ______________________________

  ____

- A report generator allows ______________________________

  ____

C. Data security [p. 10.18]

Access privileges define ______________________________

____

- With read-only privileges, you can ______________________________
- With full-update privileges, you can ______________________________

D. Backup and recovery [p. 10.18]

A DBMS provides a variety of techniques to restore a database:

- A backup is ______________________________
- A log is ______________________________

  The before image ______________________________

  The after image ______________________________
- A DBMS often provides a recovery utility to restore a database.

  In a rollback ______________________________

  In a rollforward ______________________________

VI. Relational and object-oriented databases [p. 10.19]

A data model consists of ______________________________

____

Five data models are hierarchical, network, object-relational, relational, and object-oriented.

- In a hierarchical database ______________________________

  ____

  ____

- A network database is ______________________________

  ____

- The object-relational data model combines ______________________________

  ____

A. Relational databases [p. 10.19]

A relational database stores ______________________________

____

Data Terminology:		
File Processing Developer	Relational Database Developer	Relational Database User
File	____________	____________
Record	____________	____________
Field	____________	____________

Relationships are ______________________________

1. Relational algebra [p. 10.21]

   Relational algebra uses ______________________________

   ____

   Relational operations:

   - The projection operation ______________________________
   - The selection operation ______________________________
   - The join operation ______________________________

2. Structured query language [p. 10.21]

   Structured query language (SQL) ______________________________

   ____

B. Object-oriented databases [p. 10.22]

An object-oriented database is ______________________________

____

An object is ______________________________

Advantages of an object-oriented database: ______________________________

____

Applications appropriate for an object-oriented database:

- ______________________________
- ______________________________
- ______________________________
- ______________________________

1. Object query language [p. 10.22]

   An object query language (OQL) ______________________________

   ____

VII. Database administration [p. 10.22]

A. Role of the data and database administrators [p. 10.24]

The data administrator is ______________________________

____

The database administrator is ______________________________

____

B. Role of the user [p. 10.24]

The user's responsibilities are to ______________________________

____

C. Database design guidelines: [p. 10.24]

____

____

____

____

VIII. Qualities of valuable information [p. 10.25]

Valuable information is accurate, verifiable, timely, organized, meaningful, and cost-effective:

- Accurate information is ______________________________
- Verifiable information means ______________________________
- Timely information has ______________________________
- Organized information is ______________________________
- Meaningful information is ______________________________
- Cost-effective information costs ______________________________

A. How managers use information [p. 10.25]

Managers are ______________________________

____

Management activities:

- Planning involves ______________________________

  ____
- Organizing includes ______________________________

  ____
- Leading involves ______________________________

  ____
- Controlling involves ______________________________

  ____

B. Levels of users [p. 10.26]

The type of information required often depends on a user's classification in the organization. Typically, users are classified into four levels:

1. Executive management [p. 10.26]

   Executive management ______________________________

   ____

2. Middle management [p. 10.27]

   Middle management ______________________________

   ____

3. Operational management [p. 10.27]

   Operational management ______________________________

   ____

4. Nonmanagement employees [p. 10.27]

   Nonmanagement employees ______________________________

   ____

IX. Types of information systems [p. 10.27]

An information system is ______________________________

____

Categories of information systems:

A. Office information systems [p. 10.28]

   An office information system (OIS) is ______________________________

   ____

   All levels of users benefit from an OIS.

B. Transaction processing systems [p. 10.28]

   A transaction processing system (TPS) is ______________________________

   ____

   - With batch processing ______________________________

     ____

   - With online transaction processing (OLTP) ______________________________

     ____

   Today, most transaction processing systems use OLTP.

C. Management information systems [p. 10.29]

   A management information system (MIS) is ______________________________

   ____

An MIS generates three types of information:

- Detailed information typically ______________________________

____

- Summary information consolidates ______________________________

____

- Exception information filters ______________________________

____

D. Decision support systems [p. 10.30]

A decision support system (DSS) is ______________________________

____

A DSS uses data from internal and external sources.

- Internal sources might include ______________________________

____

- External sources could include ______________________________

____

An executive information system (EIS), a special type of DSS, is __________

____

A data warehouse ______________________________

E. Expert systems [p. 10.32]

An expert system is ______________________________

____

Experts systems are composed of a knowledge base and inference rules.

- A knowledge base is ______________________________

____

- Inference rules are______________________________

____

Artificial intelligence (AI) is ______________________________

____

F. Integrated information systems [p. 10.33]

____

____

Self Test

Matching

1. ____ executive management
2. ____ middle management
3. ____ operational management
4. ____ nonmanagement employees
5. ____ office information system
6. ____ transaction processing system
7. ____ management information system
8. ____ decision support system
9. ____ executive information system
10. ____ expert system

a. a special type of DSS designed to support the information needs of senior management
b. responsible for tactical decisions that implement specific programs and plans
c. captures and stores the knowledge of human authorities and then imitates human reasoning and decision-making
d. production, clerical, and staff personnel who need frequent information to do their jobs
e. captures and processes data generated during day-to-day dealings
f. stockholders and observers responsible for investment decisions
g. generates accurate, timely, and organized information for managerial activities
h. uses hardware, software, and networks to enhance work flow and communications
i. responsible for strategic decisions that deal with overall goals and objectives
j. designed to help users reach a determination when an uncertain situation arises
k. make operational decisions that deal with an organization's day-to-day activities
l. implemented to identify errors in hardware, software, data, or procedures

True/False

____ 1. In the hierarchy of data, a field contains records, a record contains files, and a file contains databases.

____ 2. Deleting unneeded records reduces the size of files and creates additional storage space.

____ 3. Two of the advantages of file processing systems are no data redundancy and shared data.

____ 4. Database management systems are available for many sizes and types of computers.

____ 5. Report generators usually provide a means for validating data so as to reduce data entry.

____ 6. In a rollback, or backward recovery, the DBMS log is used to re-enter changes automatically since the last database save or backup.

____ 7. Because relational and object-oriented databases offer only limited data access and lack flexibility, database developers prefer two other database models: hierarchical and network.

____ 8. In addition to text hyperlinks, a hypermedia database also can contain graphics, video, and sound.

____ 9. Inaccurate information always is better than no information.

____ 10. Although expert systems can help decision-making at any level in an organization, nonmanagement employees, who utilize them to help with job-related decisions, are the primary users.

Multiple Choice

____ 1. What is the smallest unit of data that you can access?
a. a character
b. a field
c. a record
d. a file

____ 2. What does a completeness check do?
a. ensures that only the correct type of data is entered into a field
b. tests data in multiple fields to determine if a relationship is reasonable
c. determines whether a number is within a specified range
d. verifies that all required data is present

____ 3. Which of the following is *not* an advantage of the database approach?
a. reduced data redundancy
b. decreased vulnerability
c. improved data integrity
d. easier reporting

____ 4. A report generator, or report writer, is used only for what purpose?
a. to enter data
b. to change data
c. to retrieve data
d. to maintain data

____ 5. What data model organizes data in a series like a family tree or organization chart, with each child record having only one parent?
a. a hierarchical database
b. a network database
c. a relational database
d. an object-oriented database

____ 6. How does a relational database developer refer to a record?
a. as a table
b. as a relation
c. as a tuple
d. as an attribute

____ 7. In relational algebra, what operation extracts columns (fields) from a relation?
   a. the projection operation
   b. the selection operation
   c. the consistency operation
   d. the join operation

____ 8. When designing the fields for each database table, what should you *not* do?
   a. be sure each field has a unique primary key
   b. use separate fields for logically distinct items
   c. set default values for frequently entered data
   d. create fields for information that can be derived from other entries

____ 9. Activities such as recording a business activity, confirming an action or triggering a response, and maintaining data are associated with what category of information systems?
   a. office information systems (OIS)
   b. transaction processing systems (TPS)
   c. management information systems (MIS)
   d. decision support systems (DSS)

____ 10. What type of report consolidates data into a format that an individual can review quickly and easily?
   a. a detail report
   b. a projection report
   c. a summary report
   d. an exception report

Fill in the Blanks

1. A(n) ____________________ is a collection of data organized in a manner that allows access, retrieval, and use of that data.
2. ____________________ are types of files that contain applications, instructions, or documents.
3. ____________________ minimize data entry errors and thus enhance the integrity of the data before the data is stored.
4. A(n) ____________________ is a software program or set of programs designed to control access to a database and manage the data resources efficiently.
5. The capability of retrieving database information based on an instruction, called ____________________, specified by the user is a powerful database feature.
6. A(n) ____________________ is a window on the screen that provides areas for entering or changing data in a database.
7. In addition to data, a relational database stores ____________________, which are any associations among the data.
8. Some companies are developing ____________________ to take advantage of features of both the relational and object-oriented data models.

9. Transaction processing systems were developed to process business data – a function originally called ____________________.

10. ____________________ is the application of human intelligence to computers.

Complete the Table

POPULAR DATABASE MANAGEMENT SYSTEMS

Database	**Computer Type**
____________________	Handheld personal computer
Microsoft Access	____________________
____________________	Personal computer, server
Lotus Approach	____________________
Microsoft Visual FoxPro	____________________
____________________	Personal computer server, minicomputer, mainframe
DB2	____________________
____________________	Personal computer server, minicomputer, mainframe

Things to Think About

1. Why are deleted records sometimes *flagged* so they are not processed, instead of being removed immediately?
2. What type of validity check – alphabetic/numeric, completeness, range, consistency, or check digit – would be most useful when reviewing your answers on an exam? Why?
3. What characteristics of valuable information are most important? On what, if any, factors might your answer depend? Why?
4. What categories of information systems (OIS, TPS, MIS, DSS, and expert systems) would each level in an organization (executive management, middle management, operational management, and nonmanagement) be most likely to use? Why?

Puzzle

Use the given clues to complete the crossword puzzle.

Databases and Information Management

Across

1. Database model that organizes data like a family tree
6. Field that differentiates the records in a file
7. Software designed to control database access and manage data resources
9. Management activity that involves measuring performance
12. Database that stores data about engineering and scientific design
13. Type of information that typically confirms TPS activities
14. Verifies the accuracy of a primary key
17. Database model that stores data in tables consisting of rows and columns
19. Object-oriented database query language
20. Relational database query language
24. Process of comparing data to a set of rules or values to determine its accuracy
26. Relational algebra operation that retrieves certain rows based on specified criteria
27. Item that can contain both data and activities that read or manipulate the data
28. Collection of items that are not organized and have little meaning individually
29. Number, letter, punctuation mark, or symbol
30. Process used to retrieve data from a database

Down

2. Data that is organized, has meaning, and is useful
3. Check that verifies all required data is present
4. Relational algebra operation that extracts columns from a relation
5. Combination of one or more characters
8. Management activity that includes identifying and bringing together resources
10. Type of decision that deals with an organization's day-to-day activities
11. Management activity that involves instructing and authorizing others
15. Management activity that involves establishing goals and objectives
16. Database that stores images, audio clips, and/or video clips
18. Relational algebra operation that combines data from two queries
21. Database that stores schedules, calendars, manuals, memos, and reports
22. Collection of data organized in a manner that allows access, retrieval, and use
23. Group of related fields
25. Database model that allows each child record to have more than one parent record

Self Test Answers

Matching

1. *i* [p. 10.26]
2. *b* [p. 10.27]
3. *k* [p. 10.27]
4. *d* [p. 10.27]
5. *h* [p. 10.28]
6. *e* [p. 10.28]
7. *g* [p. 10.29]
8. *j* [p. 10.30]
9. *a* [p. 10.31]
0. *c* [p. 10.32]

True/False

1. *F* [p. 10.3]
2. *T* [p. 10.7]
3. *F* [p. 10.9]
4. *T* [p. 10.13]
5. *F* [p. 10.16]
6. *F* [p. 10.19]
7. *F* [p. 10.19]
8. *T* [p. 10.22]
9. *F* [p. 10.25]
0. *T* [p. 10.32]

Multiple Choice

1. *b* [p. 10.4]
2. *d* [p. 10.8]
3. *b* [p. 10.13]
4. *c* [p. 10.16]
5. *a* [p. 10.19]
6. *c* [p. 10.20]
7. *a* [p. 10.21]
8. *d* [p. 10.24]
9. *b* [p. 10.28]
0. *c* [p. 10.30]

Fill in the Blanks

1. *database* [p. 10.2]
2. *Program files* [p. 10.4]
3. *Validity checks* or *validation rules* [p. 10.7]
4. *database management system (DBMS)* [p. 10.13]
5. *criteria* [p. 10.15]
6. *form* or *data entry form* [p. 10.16]
7. *relationships* [p. 10.20]
8. *object-relational databases* [p. 10.22]
9. *data processing* [p. 10.28]
0. *Artificial intelligence (AI)* [p. 10.33]

Complete the Table

POPULAR DATABASE MANAGEMENT SYSTEMS

Database	Computer Type
Microsoft Pocket Access	Handheld personal computer
Microsoft Access	*Personal computer, server*
Corel Paradox	Personal computer, server
Lotus Approach	*Personal computer, server*
Microsoft Visual FoxPro	*Personal computer, server*

Database	**Computer Type**
Oracle	Personal computer server, minicomputer, mainframe
DB2	*Personal computer server, minicomputer, mainframe*
Informix	Personal computer server, minicomputer, mainframe

Things to Think About

Answers will vary.

Puzzle Answer

Databases and Information Management

		1 H	2 I	E	R	A	R	C	H	I	3 C	A	L				4 P		
			N								O						R		5 F
6 K	E	Y	F	I	E	L	D		7 D	B	M	S			8 O		O		I
			O								P				R		J		E
			R		9 C	10 O	N	T	R	O	L	L	I	N	G		E		L
	11 L		M			P					E				A		12 C	A	D
13 D	E	T	A	I	L	E	D				T				N		T		
	A		T			R			14 C	H	E	C	K	D	I	G	I	T	
	D		I			A					N				Z		O		15 P
	I		O			T		16 M		17 R	E	L	A	T	I	O	N	A	L
	N		N			I		U			S				N				A
	G			18 J		19 O	Q	L			20 S	Q	L		G		21 G		N
		22 D		O		N		T						23 R			R		N
	24 V	A	L	I	D	A	T	I	O	N		25 N		E			O		I
		T		N		L		M				E		C			U		N
		A					26 S	E	L	E	C	T	I	O	N		P		G
	27 O	B	J	E	C	T		D				W		R			W		
		A						I				O		28 D	A	T	A		
		S		29 C	H	A	R	A	C	T	E	R					R		
		E										K			30 Q	U	E	R	Y

DISCOVERING COMPUTERS 2000

STUDY GUIDE

CHAPTER 11

Information Systems Development

Chapter Overview

This chapter explores information systems development and traces the development process in Manhattan Construction, a fictional company. You are introduced to the system development life cycle (SDLC) and discover the phases in the SDLC. Guidelines for system development, participants in the system development life cycle, project management, feasibility assessment, documentation, and data and information gathering techniques are reviewed. You learn what initiates the system development life cycle. Aspects of the planning phase and analysis phase are described. You investigate the many activities in the design phase and explore the various tasks in the implementation phase. Finally, you learn the purpose of the support phase.

Chapter Objectives

After completing this chapter, you should be able to:

- Explain the phases in the system development life cycle
- Identify the guidelines for system development
- Discuss the importance of project management, feasibility assessment, data and information gathering techniques, and documentation
- Describe how structured tools such as entity-relationship diagrams and data flow diagrams are used in analysis and design
- Differentiate between packaged software and custom software
- Identify program development as part of the system development life cycle
- Discuss techniques used to convert to a new system and support an information system

Chapter Outline

I. What is the system development life cycle? [p. 11.2]

The system development life cycle (SDLC) is ______________________________

____

A. Phases in the SDLC [p. 11.2]

The system development life cycle can be grouped into these phases:

1. ________________ 3. ________________ 5. ________________

2. ________________ 4. ________________

The phases form a loop; that is, information system development is an ongoing process.

B. Guidelines for system development [p. 11.3]

Information system development should follow three guidelines:

(1) ____

(2) ____

Users include ____

(3) ____

Standards are ____

C. Who participates in the system development life cycle? [p. 11.3]

A systems analyst is ____

____

A programmer uses ____

____

The steering committee is ____

A project team is established to ____

The project leader ____

D. Project management [p. 11.4]

Project management is ____

____

The project leader must identify:

- ____
- ____
- ____
- ____
- ____
- ____

The project leader usually records the above items in a project plan.

- A Gantt chart is ____

  ____

- A deliverable is ____

  ____

E. Feasibility assessment [p. 11.5]

Feasibility is ______________________________

____

Criteria used to test project feasibility:

- Operational feasibility measures ______________________________

  ____

- Schedule feasibility measures ______________________________

  ____

- Technical feasibility measures ______________________________

  ____

- Economic feasibility measures ______________________________

  ____

F. Documentation [p. 11.6]

Documentation is ______________________________

____

A project notebook stores ______________________________

A project dictionary is ______________________________

Well-written, ongoing, thorough documentation makes it easier to understand all aspects of the SDLC and to modify the system to meet changing needs.

G. Data and information gathering techniques [p. 11.7]

Techniques used during the SDLC to gather data and information:

- ______________________________
- ______________________________
- ______________________________
- ______________________________

  In an unstructured interview ______________________________

  In a structured interview ______________________________

- ______________________________
- ______________________________

II. What initiates the system development life cycle? [p. 11.8]

A user may request a new or modified information system for external reasons (e.g., to respond to competitors) or internal reasons (e.g., to correct a problem).

A request for system services, or project request, is a standard form that documents the request and becomes ______________________________

____

III. Planning phase [p. 11.11]

The planning phase begins when ______________________________

Major activities during the planning phase:

(1) ______________________________

(2) ______________________________

(3) ______________________________

(4) ______________________________

IV. Analysis phase [p. 11.12]

The analysis phase consists of two major tasks:

(1) ______________________________

(2) ______________________________

A. The preliminary investigation [p. 11.12]

The preliminary investigation is to ______________________________

____

A feasibility report presents the results of the preliminary investigation.

The most important aspect of the preliminary investigation is______________

____

B. Detailed analysis [p. 11.14]

Detailed analysis involves three major activities:

(1) ______________________________

(2) ______________________________

(3) ______________________________

Detailed analysis sometimes is called logical design because ______________

____

During detailed analysis, all of the data and information gathering techniques are used.

C. Structured analysis and design tools [p. 11.15]

Structured analysis and design ______________________________

____

Structured analysis and design tools:

1. Entity-relationship diagrams [p. 11.15]

An entity is ______________________________

An entity-relationship diagram (ERD) is ______________________________

____

2. Data flow diagrams [p. 11.16]
   A data flow diagram (DFD) is ______________________________

   ____

   Components of a DFD:
   - A data flow ______________________________
   - A process ______________________________
   - A data store ______________________________
   - A source ______________________________
3. Project dictionary [p. 11.17]
   The project dictionary contains ______________________________

   ____

   In the project dictionary, entries from DFDs and ERDs are described using several techniques, including structured English, decision tables and decision trees, and the data dictionary.
4. Structured English [p. 11.17]
   Structured English is ______________________________

   ____
5. Decision tables and decision trees [p. 11.18]
   A decision table is ______________________________

   ____

   A decision tree is ______________________________
6. Data dictionary [p. 11.19]
   The data dictionary section of the project dictionary stores ______________

   ____

D. The build-or-buy decision [p. 11.19]
   The system proposal ______________________________

   ____

   In a build-or-buy decision, an organization decides ______________________

   ____

   1. Packaged software [p. 11.20]
      Packaged software is ______________________________

      ____

      - Horizontal application software ______________________
      - Vertical application software ______________________

2. Custom software [p. 11.20]
   Custom software is ______________________________
   ____

V. Design phase [p. 11.21]

The design phase consists of two major activities:

(1) ______________________________

(2) ______________________________

A. Acquiring necessary hardware and software [p. 11.21]

Acquiring the necessary hardware and software consists of four tasks:

(1) ______________________________

(2) ______________________________

(3) ______________________________

(4) ______________________________

B. Identifying technical specifications [p. 11.21]

A systems analyst identifies hardware, software, and networking requirements. Technical requirements are summarized in an RFQ or RFP.

- A request for quotation (RFQ) is ______________________________
  ____
- A request for proposal (RFP) is ______________________________
  ____
- A request for information (RFI) is ______________________________
  ____

C. Soliciting vendor proposals [p. 11.22]

With an RFQ or RFP, proposals can be solicited from vendors on the Internet, local computer stores, computer manufacturers, or value-added resellers.

A value-added reseller (VAR) is ______________________________
____

A consultant ______________________________

D. Testing and evaluating vendor proposals [p. 11.22]

Vendor proposals should be rated as objectively as possible.

A benchmark test measures ______________________________

E. Making a decision [p. 11.24]

After rating proposals, the systems analyst makes a recommendation to the steering committee. A contract then can be awarded to a vendor.

An end-user license agreement is ______________________________

F. Detailed design [p. 11.24]

Detailed design sometimes is called physical design because ______________

____

Designs are developed for databases, inputs and outputs, and programs.

1. Database design [p. 11.25]

   During database design, the systems analyst ______________________

   ____

2. Input and output design [p. 11.26]

   During input and output design, the systems analyst ________________

   ____

   - A mockup ______________________________________
   - A layout chart __________________________________

3. Program design [p. 11.27]

   During program design, the systems analyst ______________________

   ____

   - The program specification package ___________________

     ____

   - A systems flowchart shows _________________________

     ____

G. Prototyping [p. 11.27]

A prototype is ____

H. CASE tools [p. 11.28]

Computer-aided software engineering (CASE) products are ______________

____

Capabilities of I-CASE (integrated CASE) products:

- ______________________ • ______________________
- ______________________ • ______________________
- ______________________ • ______________________

I. Quality review techniques [p. 11.29]

A structured walkthrough is _________________________________

____

VI. Implementation phase [p. 11.29]

The purpose of the implementation phase is ________________________

____

Four major activities are performed in the implementation phase:

(1) ____________________

(2) ____________________

(3) ____________________

(4) ____________________

A. Develop programs [p. 11.29]

Custom software can be developed from the specifications created during analysis. The program development life cycle (PDLC) follows six steps:

(1) ____________________ (4) ____________________

(2) ____________________ (5) ____________________

(3) ____________________ (6) ____________________

The PDLC is part of ____________________

B. Install and test the new system [p. 11.29]

Types of tests performed to test the new system:

- Systems test: ____________________
- Integration test: ____________________
- Acceptance test: ____________________

C. Train and educate users [p. 11.30]

Training involves ____________________

Education is ____________________

D. Convert to the new system [p. 11.30]

Conversion can take place using the following strategies:

- With direct conversion ____________________
- Parallel conversion consists of ____________________
- Phased conversion is ____________________
- With a pilot conversion ____________________

VII. Support phase [p. 11.31]

The purpose of the support phase is ____

____

The support phase consists of four major activities:

(1) ____

(2) ____

(3) ____

(4) ____

The post-implementation system review is ______________________________

____

System enhancement involves ______________________________________

____

Performance monitoring is ____

____

Self Test

Matching

1. ____ SDLC
2. ____ ERD
3. ____ DFD
4. ____ RFQ
5. ____ RFP
6. ____ RFI
7. ____ VAR
8. ____ RAD
9. ____ CASE
10. ____ PDLC

a. organized set of six activities in the creation of a computer program
b. standard form sent to vendors to request information about a product or service
c. company that purchases products and resells them along with additional services
d. organized set of activities that guides users through information system development
e. process that often uses prototypes to develop applications throughout the SDLC
f. license agreement granting the right to use software under certain terms and conditions
g. tool that represents graphically the flow of data in a system
h. sent to vendors to request prices for specified products
i. tabular representation of actions to be taken given various conditions
j. computer-based tools designed to support activities of the SDLC
k. tool that graphically represents associations between entities in a project
l. asks vendors to select products that meet your requirements and then quote prices

True/False

____ 1. The goal of project management is to deliver an acceptable system to the user in an agreed-upon time frame, while maintaining costs.

____ 2. Documentation should be an ongoing part of the system development life cycle.

____ 3. Unstructured interviews tend to be more successful for the systems analyst.

____ 4. The perceived problem or enhancement identified in the project request always is the actual problem.

____ 5. An important benefit from studying the existing system and determining user requirements is that these activities build valuable relationships among the systems analyst and users.

____ 6. Lower-level data flow diagrams (DFDs) identify only the major process; that is, the system being studied.

____ 7. Vertical application software packages tend to be widely available because they can be used by a greater number of organizations; thus, they usually are less expensive than horizontal application software packages.

____ 8. The advantage of a full-scale VAR (value-added reseller) is that you deal with only one company for an entire system.

____ 9. The main advantage of a prototype is that users can work with the system before it is completed – to make sure it meets their needs.

____ 10. Errors in an information system may be caused by problems with design (logic) or programming (syntax).

Multiple Choice

____ 1. Which of the following is *not* a general guideline for system development?
   a. set appropriate constraints
   b. use a phased approach
   c. involve the users
   d. develop standards

____ 2. What criteria that tests the feasibility of a project addresses the question of whether users will like the new system?
   a. cost/benefit feasibility
   b. technical feasibility
   c. schedule feasibility
   d. operational feasibility

____ 3. What is an internal reason for changing an information system?
   a. mandates by a governing body
   b. competition from other organizations
   c. a desire to improve or enhance the current system
   d. all of the above

____ 4. The preliminary investigation is a major task in what phase?
   a. analysis
   b. planning
   c. design
   d. implementation

____ 5. In a data flow diagram, what is drawn as a rounded rectangle?
   a. a data flow
   b. a process
   c. a data store
   d. a source

____ 6. What technique graphically represents the actions to be taken given various conditions?
a. a project dictionary
b. a decision table
c. a data dictionary
d. a decision tree

____ 7. What is the main advantage of custom software?
a. it matches an organization's requirements exactly
b. it is less expensive than packaged software
c. it takes less time to design than packaged software
d. it takes less time to implement than packaged software

____ 8. What do most end-user license agreements state?
a. software may be used on more than one computer or by more than one user
b. software may not be used on more than one computer, but it can be used by more than one user
c. software may be used on more than one computer but not by more than one user
d. software may not be used on more than one computer or by more than one user

____ 9. What capabilities do I-CASE products include?
a. a graphics facility that enables the drawing of diagrams
b. a quality insurance facility to analyze deliverables
c. code generators that create actual programs
d. all of the above

____ 10. An accounting system, with the accounts receivable, accounts payable, general ledger, and payroll sites all being converted in separate stages, would be an example of what kind of conversion?
a. direct conversion
b. parallel conversion
c. phased conversion
d. pilot conversion

Fill in the Blanks

1. The many activities of the SDLC are grouped into five larger categories called ____________________.

2. To plan and schedule a project effectively, the project leader must identify the ____________________; that is, the project's goal, objectives, and expectations.

3. A form called a(n) ____________________ becomes the first item of documentation in the project notebook.

4. A report called a(n) ____________________ compiles the results of a very general preliminary investigation.

5. In a data flow diagram, a(n) ____________________ is drawn as a square and identifies an entity outside the scope of the system that sends data into the system or receives information from the system.
6. The goal of the ____________________ is to assess the feasibility of each alternative solution and then recommend the most feasible solution for the development project.
7. ____________________ is application software developed by the user or at the user's request.
8. A(n) ____________________ is a guarantee that a product will function properly for a specified period of time.
9. Many companies use ____________________, which involves users in maintaining the quality in a system.
10. Converting existing manual and computer-based files so they can be used by a new system is called ____________________

Complete the Table

CONVERTING TO A NEW SYSTEM

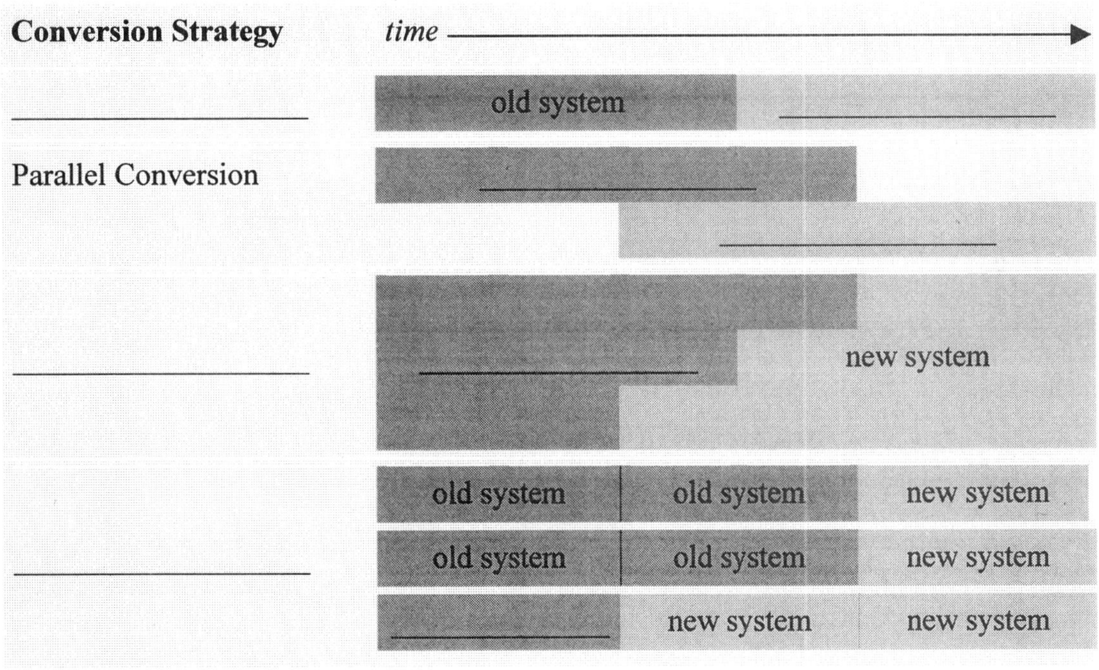

Conversion Strategy	*time* →		
____________________	old system	____________________	
Parallel Conversion	____________________		
		____________________	
____________________	____________________	new system	
____________________	old system	old system	new system
	old system	old system	new system
	____________________	new system	new system

Things to Think About

1. Why does the start of many activities in the system development life cycle depend on the successful completion of other activities?
2. Although they are created in the analysis phase, how might the project dictionary and data dictionary be used in subsequent phases of the system development life cycle?

3. If an organization chooses to buy packaged software, why might it have to change some of its methods and procedures? When might custom software be worth the additional cost and development time?
4. How can untrained users prevent the estimated benefits of a new system from ever being obtained or, worse, contribute to less efficiency and more costs than when the old system was operational?

Puzzle

Write the word described by each clue in the puzzle below. Words can be written forward or backward, across, up and down, or diagonally. The initial letter of each word already appears in the puzzle.

	E										D
F		A					S				
	U	S	E			P			D	P	
				C							
								P			
					P						
			G		L						
	P							M			
							W				S

organized set of activities that guides people through the development of an information system

include anyone for whom an information system is being built

sets of rules and procedures that an organization expects employees to accept and follow

writes the instructions that direct a computer to process data into information

type of chart that uses horizontal bars to represent project phases or activities

any tangible item

measurement of how suitable the development of a system will be

phase that begins when the steering committee receives a project request

phase that consists of two major tasks

tool that graphically represents associations between objects about which data is stored

tool that graphically represents the flow of data

represented by a line with an arrow in a DFD

graphical representation of actions to be taken given various conditions

type of software that already is developed for purchase

type of software developed by the user or at the user's request

guarantee that a product will function properly for a specified time period

sample of input or output that contains actual data

organized set of activities in the development of a computer program

the process of learning new principles or theories that helps users understand a system

phase that provides ongoing assistance for an information system and its users after it is implemented

Self Test Answers

Matching

1. *d* [p. 11.2]
2. *k* [p. 11.15]
3. *g* [p. 11.16]
4. *h* [p. 11.22]
5. *l* [p. 11.22]
6. *b* [p. 11.22]
7. *c* [p. 11.22]
8. *e* [p. 11.27]
9. *j* [p. 11.28]
0. *a* [p. 11.29]

True/False

1. *T* [p. 11.4]
2. *T* [p. 11.6]
3. *F* [p. 11.7]
4. *F* [p. 11.13]
5. *T* [p. 11.15]
6. *F* [p. 11.16]
7. *F* [p. 11.20]
8. *T* [p. 11.22]
9. *T* [p. 11.27]
0. *T* [p. 11.31]

Multiple Choice

1. *a* [p. 11.3]
2. *d* [p. 11.5]
3. *c* [p. 11.9]
4. *a* [p. 11.12]
5. *b* [p. 11.16]
6. *d* [p. 11.18]
7. *a* [p. 11.20]
8. *d* [p. 11.24]
9. *d* [p. 11.28]
0. *c* [p. 11.30]

Fill in the Blanks

1. *phases* [p. 11.2]
2. *scope* [p. 11.4]
3. *request for system services* or *project request* [p. 11.9]
4. *feasibility study* or *feasibility report* [p. 11.12]
5. *source* or *agent* [p. 11.16]
6. *system proposal* [p. 11.19]
7. *Custom software* [p. 11.20]
8. *warranty* [p. 11.22]
9. *total quality management (TQM)* [p. 11.30]
0. *data conversion* [p. 11.30]

Complete the Table

CONVERTING TO A NEW SYSTEM

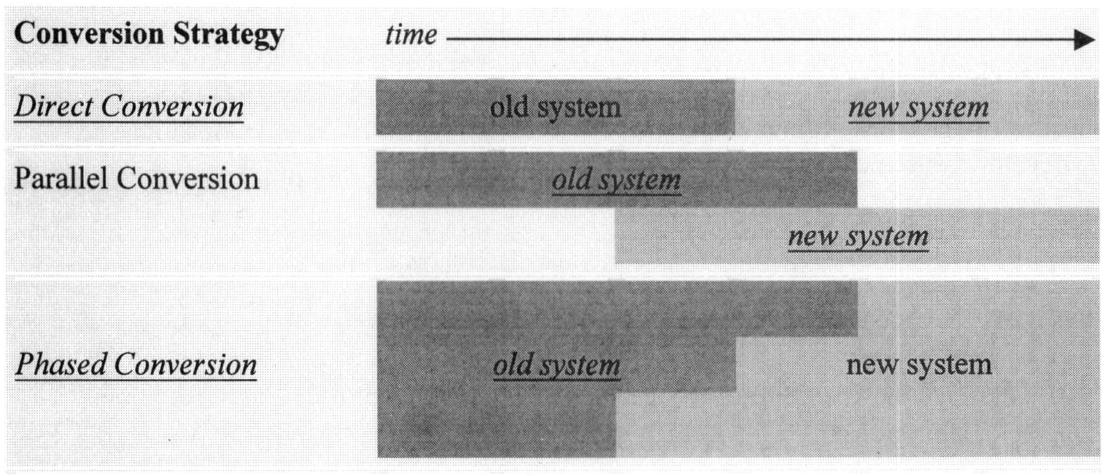

Conversion Strategy	*time* →		
	old system	old system	new system
<u>*Pilot Conversion*</u>	old system	old system	new system
	<u>*new system*</u>	new system	new system

Things to Think About

Answers will vary.

Puzzle Answer

E	**E**	R	T	N	O	I	S	I	C	E	**D**
F	D	**A**	N	A	L	Y	**S**	I	S	F	E
E	**U**	**S**	**E**	R	S	**P**	T	C	**D**	**P**	L
A	C	U	R	**C**	S	L	A	L	A	A	I
S	A	P	D	U	E	A	N	D	T	C	V
I	T	P	T	S	C	N	D	**P**	A	K	E
B	I	O	T	T	O	N	A	U	F	A	R
I	O	R	N	O	R	I	R	K	L	G	A
L	N	T	A	M	**P**	N	D	C	O	E	B
I	C	I	**G**	O	**L**	G	S	O	W	D	L
T	**P**	R	O	G	R	A	M	**M**	E	R	E
Y	T	N	A	R	R	A	**W**	C	L	D	**S**

DISCOVERING COMPUTERS 2000

STUDY GUIDE

CHAPTER 12

Program Development and Programming Languages

Chapter Overview

This chapter examines program development and programming languages. You learn what a computer program is and examine the six steps in the program development life cycle: analyze problem, design programs, code programs, test programs, formalize solution, and maintain programs. Program design concepts and tools are introduced. Programming language is defined, and the categories of programming languages – machine languages, assembly languages, third-generation languages, fourth-generation languages, and natural languages – are identified. You explore object-oriented program development and discover popular programming languages. Program development tools are described, and Web page program development and techniques are presented. Finally, multimedia program development is explained and factors to consider when selecting a programming language are presented.

Chapter Objectives

After completing this chapter, you should be able to:

- Explain the six steps in the program development life cycle
- Describe top-down program design
- Explain structured program design and the three basic control structures
- Explain the differences among the categories of programming languages
- Describe the object-oriented approach to program development
- Identify programming languages commonly used today
- Identify the uses of application generators, macros, and RAD tools
- Describe various Web page development tools, including HTML, DHTML, and XML

Chapter Outline

I. What is a computer program? [p. 12.2]

A computer program is ____

____

A programming language is ____

____

II. The program development life cycle [p. 12.2]

The program development life cycle (PDLC) is______________________________

____

The PDLC consists of six steps:

1. ____________________ 3. ____________________ 5. ____________________

2. ____________________ 4. ____________________ 6. ____________________

The phases form a loop; that is, program development is an ongoing process within the SDLC.

A. What initiates the program development life cycle? [p. 12.3]

Requests for a new or modified program usually are made at ______________

____

If a company opts for in-house development, the design phase of the SDLC focuses on developing a program specification package, which is __________

____

The programming team ____

By following the steps in the PDLC, programmers can create programs that are ____

III. Step 1 – Analyze problem [p. 12.4]

The first step in the PDLC is to ____

____

The analysis step consists of three major tasks:

(1) ____

(2) ____

(3) ____

An IPO chart identifies ____

____

IV. Step 2 – Design programs [p. 12.5]

Designing programs involves three tasks:

(1) ____

(2) ____

(3) ____

A. Top-down design [p. 12.5]

Top-down design breaks ______________________________

____

A module is ______________________________

A hierarchy chart is used to ______________________________

B. Structured design [p. 12.6]

The solution algorithm is ______________________________

____

Structured design is ______________________________

____

A control structure is ______________________________

____

Structured design uses three basic control structures:

1. Sequence control structure [p. 12.6]

   A sequence control structure shows ______________________________

   ____

2. Selection control structure [p. 12.6]

   A selection control structure tells ______________________________

   ____

   - In an if-then-else control structure ______________________________

     ____

   - The case control structure ______________________________

     ____

3. The repetition control structure [p. 12.7]

   The repetition control structure is ______________________________

   ____

   - The do-while control structure ______________________________

     ____

   - The do-until control structure ______________________________

     ____

C. Proper program design [p. 12.8]

With top-down and structured techniques, programmers must ensure that programs adhere to proper program design rules. A proper program has:

1. No dead code

   Dead code is ______________________________

2. No infinite loops

   An infinite loop is ______________________________

3. One entry point

   An entry point is ______________________________

4. One exit point

   An exit point is ______________________________

D. Design tools [p. 12.9]

Design tools are used by programmers to help develop a solution algorithm.

Three commonly-used design tools:

1. Program flowchart [p. 12.9]

   A program flowchart ______________________________

   ____

2. Nassi-Schneiderman chart [p. 12.10]

   A Nassi-Schneiderman (N-S) chart ______________________________

   ____

3. Pseudocode [p. 12.11]

   Pseudocode ______________________________

   ____

E. Quality review techniques [p. 12.12]

During a quality review, the programmer ______________________________

____

A logic error is ______________________________

- Desk checking is ______________________________

  ____

  Test data is ______________________________

- A structured walkthrough ______________________________

  ____

V. Step 3 – Code programs [p. 12.13]

Coding programs involves two steps:

(1) ______________________________

(2) ______________________________

Syntax is ______________________________

Comments are ______________________________

VI. Step 4 – Test programs [p. 12.13]

The goal of program testing is ______________________________

____

Errors usually are one of two types:

(1) ______________ (2) ______________

A syntax error occurs when ______________________________

Debugging is ______________________________

A debug utility ______________________________

The Millenium Bug ______________________________

VII. Step 5 – Formalize solution [p. 12.14]

In formalizing the solution, the programmer performs two activities:

(1) ______________________________

(2) ______________________________

VIII. Step 6 – Maintain programs [p. 12.15]

Maintaining programs involves:

(1) ______________________________

(2) ______________________________

Program enhancement involves ______________________________

____

IX. Programming languages and program development tools [p. 12.15]

A programming language is ______________________________

____

A program development tool consists of ______________________________

____

X. Categories of programming languages [p. 12.15]

The American National Standards Institute (ANSI) has ______________

____

- A low-level language is ______________________________

  Machine and assembly languages are low-level languages.
- A high-level language can ______________________________

  Third-generation, fourth-generation, and natural languages are high-level languages.

A. Machine languages [p. 12.16]

Machine language is ____

____

Machine language programs are machine-dependant; that is, they run only on the computer for which they were developed.

B. Assembly languages [p. 12.16]

With an assembly language ____

____

Symbolic instruction codes are ____

____

The source program is ____

An assembler converts ____

____

C. Third-generation languages [p. 12.17]

High-level languages are machine-independent, meaning ____________________

____

A third-generation language (3GL) instruction is ____________________

____

3GLs are called procedural languages because ____________________

____

3GL source programs are translated using one of two types of programs:

- A compiler converts ____

  ____

  The object code is ____
- An interpreter translates ____

  ____

D. Fourth-generation languages [p. 12.18]

A fourth-generation language (4GL) is ____________________

____

A 4GL is a nonprocedural language, which means ____________________

____

Many 4GLs work in combination with a database and project dictionary. SQL (Structured Query Language) is a popular ANSI-standard 4GL that enables users and programmers to ____

A report writer is ____

____

E. Natural languages [p. 12.19]

A natural language is ______________________________

____

XI. Object-oriented program development [p. 12.19]

With the object-oriented approach, the programmer can ______________________________

____

An object is ______________________________

- Methods ______________________________
- Attributes ______________________________

Encapsulation is ______________________________

A class is ______________________________

- Subclasses ______________________________
- A superclass ______________________________

Inheritance is ______________________________

An object instance is ______________________________

A message tells ______________________________

A major benefit of the object-oriented approach is the ability to reuse and modify existing objects.

A. Object-oriented programming [p. 12.20]

An object-oriented programming (OOP) language is ______________________________

____

Event is ______________________________

XII. Popular programming languages [p. 12.21]

Although there are hundreds of programming languages, only a few are widely used. Most are high-level languages that work on a variety of machines.

A. BASIC [p. 12.21]

____

____

B. Visual Basic [p. 12.22]

____

____

C. COBOL [p. 12.23]

____

____

D. C [p. 12.23]

E. C++ [p. 12.23]

F. FORTRAN [p. 12.24]

G. Pascal [p. 12.25]

H. Ada [p. 12.25]

I. RPG [p. 12.26]

J. Other programming languages [p. 12.26]

XIII. Program development tools [p. 12.27]

Program development tools are

In addition to query languages and report writers, program development tools include application generators, macros, and RAD tools.

A. Application generators [p. 12.27]

An application generator is

A menu generator allows

B. Macros [p. 12.28]

A macro is

You usually create a macro in one of two ways:

(1) ______________________________

A macro recorder is ______________________________

(2) ______________________________

Visual Basic is a popular macro programming language.

C. RAD tools: Visual Basic, Delphi, and PowerBuilder [p. 12.29]

Rapid application development (RAD) is ______________________________

____

Prototyping is a common approach used in RAD.

A prototype is ______________________________

Popular RAD tools:

1. Visual Basic [p. 12.29]

   ____

2. Delphi [p. 12.29]

   ____

3. PowerBuilder [p. 12.29]

   ____

XIV. Web page program development [p. 12.29]

Web page authors ______________________________

____

A. HTML [p. 12.30]

Hypertext markup language (HTML) is ______________________________

____

Tags are ______________________________

- A stand-alone HTML editor is ______________________________
- An add-on HTML editor is ______________________________

B. Scripts, applets, and servlets [p. 12.31]

To add dynamic content and interactive elements to Web pages, you develop small programs in the form of scripts, applets, and servlets.

- A script is ______________________________
- An applet usually ______________________________
- A servlet is ______________________________

Common gateway interface (CGI) is ______________________________

____

Ways of transferring information to and from a Web server:

- A counter tracks ______
- An image map is ______
- A processing form collects ______

C. Java, JavaScript, and Perl [p. 12.32]

1. Java [p. 12.32]

   Java is ______

   ______

2. JavaScript [p. 12.33]

   JavaScript is ______

   ______

3. Perl [p. 12.33]

   Perl is ______

   ______

D. Dynamic HTML [p. 12.34]

Dynamic HTML (DHTML) is ______

______

In addition to basic HTML and scripting languages, DHTML includes:

- The document object model (DOM) defines ______
- A style sheet contains ______

E. XML [p. 12.35]

eXtensible Markup Language (XML) ______

______

XV. Multimedia Program Development [p. 12.35]

Multimedia authoring software is ______

______

XVI. Selecting a programming language or program development tool [p. 12.35]

Factors to consider:

1. ______
2. ______
3. ______
4. ______

Self Test

Matching

1. ____ BASIC
2. ____ Visual Basic
3. ____ COBOL
4. ____ C
5. ____ FORTRAN
6. ____ Pascal
7. ____ Ada
8. ____ RPG
9. ____ Java
10. ____ Perl

a. simple, interactive, problem-solving language often used in introductory courses
b. nonprocedural language used for generating reports and updating files
c. scientific language designed to manipulate tables of numbers
d. object-oriented language developed by Apple to manipulate multimedia cards
e. Windows-based application designed to assist in developing event-driven applications
f. interpreted scripting language, especially designed for processing text
g. one of the first high-level languages; originally intended for scientific applications
h. widely used procedural language for business applications; easy to read, write, and maintain
i. originally designed as a language to write systems software, used most often with UNIX
j. compiled object-oriented language used to write applications, applets, and servlets
k. language developed for the purpose of teaching structured programming concepts
l. language originally designed to meet the needs of embedded computer systems

True/False

____ 1. Programs developed using the top-down approach suffer from the complexity of their design – they usually are unstable and difficult to read and maintain.

____ 2. Unlike a do-while control structure that continues to loop *until* the condition is true, a do-until control structure continues to loop *while* the condition is true – and then stops.

____ 3. Prior to the introduction of proper program design, poorly designed programs sometimes were called *spaghetti code*.

____ 4. During program testing, one purpose of using test data is to try to *crash* the system; that is, try to make it fail.

____ 5. As with machine languages, assembly languages usually are easy to learn and are machine-independent.

____ 6. While a compiler translates one program statement at a time, an interpreter translates an entire program at once.

____ 7. When using an application generator, the developer (a programmer or user) works with menu-driven tools that have graphical user interfaces.

____ 8. Many applications use Visual Basic or a similar language as their macro programming language.

____ 9. Scripts, applets, and servlets are long programs that are executed by the operating system – unlike regular programs, which are executed inside of another program.

____ 10. A Web page written with XML probably would require multiple versions to run on a handheld computer, a laptop computer, and a desktop computer.

Multiple Choice

____ 1. Preparing the program specification package is the last activity in what phase of the system development life cycle?
   a. the planning phase
   b. the analysis phase
   c. the design phase
   d. the implementation phase

____ 2. What is the first step in top-down design?
   a. identify the major function of the program
   b. break down the program's main routine into smaller sections
   c. identify the minor functions of the program
   d. combine the program's smaller sections into a main routine

____ 3. Which of the following is *not* a commonly used program design tool?
   a. program flowcharts
   b. Nassi-Schneiderman charts
   c. pseudocode
   d. debug utilities

____ 4. In correct sequence, what are the steps in desk checking?
   a. determine the expected result, develop test data, compare the expected result to the actual result, step through the solution algorithm using test data and write down the actual result
   b. develop test data, step through the solution algorithm using test data and write down the actual result, determine the expected result, compare the expected result to the actual result
   c. determine the expected result, step through the solution algorithm using test data and write down the actual result, compare the expected result to the actual result, develop test data
   d. develop test data, determine the expected result, step through the solution algorithm using test data and write down the actual result, compare the expected result to the actual result

____ 5. What major category of programming languages uses a series of binary digits (1s and 0s) that correspond to the on and off electrical states of a computer?
a. machine languages
b. assembly languages
c. third-generation languages
d. natural languages

____ 6. What major category of programming languages often is associated with expert systems and artificial intelligence?
a. third-generation languages
b. natural languages
c. fourth-generation languages
d. assembly languages

____ 7. What is C++?
a. a language similar to C used for device control applications
b. an object-oriented extension of C used to develop application software
c. a successor to C used for artificial intelligence applications
d. an enhanced version of C with features of FORTRAN and COBOL

____ 8. Although a version with limited functionality is available for the personal computer, what programming language primarily is used for application development on IBM midrange computers?
a. BASIC
b. COBOL
c. FORTRAN
d. RPG

____ 9. What are <B> to bold text, <P> to indicate a new paragraph, and <HR> to display a horizontal rule across a page?
a. scripts
b. applets
c. tags
d. servlets

____ 10. What is *not* a factor that should be considered when selecting a programming language?
a. standards of the organization
b. need for testing and documentation
c. suitability of the language to the application
d. portability to other systems

Fill in the Blanks

1. In a program flowchart, dotted lines are used to connect ____________________, which explain or clarify logic in the algorithm.
2. Today, programmers use ____________________ to develop flowcharts, which makes these flowcharts easy to modify and update.

3. In pseudocode, you identify control structures by their ____________________: the actions within a module are moved in from the left margin
4. The errors in a program are referred to as ____________________.
5. Once programs are ____________________, or placed into production, users interact with the programs to process real, or *live*, transactions.
6. An advantage of assembly languages is that the programmer can refer to storage locations with ____________________.
7. In some cases, assembly languages include ____________________, which generate more than one machine instruction.
8. SQL is a(n) ____________________ enabling users to retrieve data from database tables.
9. Because encapsulation conceals the details of an object, it sometimes is called ____________________.
10. Program development tools ____________________ nontechnical users by giving these users the ability to write simple programs and satisfy information processing requests on their own.

Complete the Table

STANDARD SYMBOLS USED TO CREATE PROGRAM FLOWCHARTS

Symbol	Operation	Purpose
[rectangle]	________________	Program instruction(s) that transforms input(s) into output(s)
________________	INPUT/OUTPUT	________________________________
[diamond]	________________	Condition that determines a specified path to follow
________________	TERMINAL	________________________________
[circle]	________________	Entry from or exit to another part of the flowchart on the same page
[rectangle with double vertical sides]	________________	Named process containing a series of specified program steps

Things to Think About

1. Why should a programmer not change design specifications without the agreement of the systems analyst and the user?
2. Prior to the introduction of structured program design, programmers focused on the detailed steps required for a program and logical solutions for each new combination of conditions as it was encountered. Why would developing programs in this manner lead to poorly designed programs?
3. Why is it better to find errors and make needed changes to a program during the design step than to make them later in the development process?
4. Would it be more difficult to uncover syntax errors or logic errors in a program? Why?

Puzzle

The terms described by the phrases below are written below each line in code. Break the code by writing the correct term above the coded word. Then, use your broken code to translate the final sentence.

1. set of instructions that directs the computer to perform tasks to process data into information — EJGCWMZD CDJUDHG
2. identifies the inputs to a program, the outputs generated, and the processing steps required — IZOSBSBU ISHUDHG
3. used by programmers to represent program modules graphically — MJC-IJRB EYHDM
4. graphical or written description of the step-by-step procedures for a module — CDJUDHG VJUSE
5. design that controls the logical order in which program instructions are executed — EJBQMDWEM
6. type of control structure that shows a single action, or a single action followed by another action — QZXWZBEZ
7. type of control structure used when an action is to be repeated as long as a certain condition is met — SMZDHMSJB
8. what Nassi-Schneiderman (N-S) charts sometimes are called — QMDWEMWDZI OVJREYHDMQ
9. documentation within a program — DZGHDFQ
10. allows you to identify syntax errors and find logic errors while a program runs in slow motion — IZAWUUZD
11. error found in many computers at the turn of the century — P2F AWU
12. meaningful abbreviations for assembly language program instructions — GBZGJBSEQ
13. software that enables a developer to design or layout a report on the screen — DZCJDM UZBZDHMJD
14. in the object-oriented approach, the procedures in an object — JCZDHMSJBQ
15. in the object-oriented approach, the data elements in an object — KHDSHAVZQ
16. development tool that allows you to build an application without writing extensive code — CDJUDHG UZBZDHMJD

17. HTML codes that specify links to other documents and how a Web page displays — GHDFWCQ
18. collects data from visitors to a Web site, who fill in blank fields — CDJEZQQSBU OJDG
19. simple, open scripting language that anyone can use without purchasing a license — THKHQEDSCM
20. Web page development language that some experts predict will replace HTML — ZLMZBQSAVZ GHDFWC

MJ VWDZ ZLCZDM CDJUDHGGZDQ, SB HIISMSJB MJ YSUY QHVHDSZQ HBI

QSUBSBU AJBWQZQ QJGZ EJGCHBSZQ HDZ JOOZDSBU QWEY CZDFQ HQ

OVZLSAVZ YJWDQ, IHP EHDZ, OHGSVP VZHKZ, QMJEF JCMSJBQ, RJDFCVHEZ

OSMBZQQ EZBMZDQ, HBI ZKZB QWAQSISNZI VHWBIDP QZDKSEZ.

Self Test Answers

Matching

1. *a* [p. 12.21]
2. *e* [p. 12.22]
3. *h* [p. 12.23]
4. *i* [p. 12.23]
5. *g* [p. 12.24]
6. *k* [p. 12.25]
7. *l* [p. 12.25]
8. *b* [p. 12.26]
9. *j* [p. 12.32]
0. *f* [p. 12.33]

True/False

1. *F* [p. 12.5]
2. *F* [p. 12.7]
3. *T* [p. 12.9]
4. *T* [p. 12.14]
5. *F* [p. 12.16]
6. *F* [p. 12.18]
7. *T* [p. 12.27]
8. *T* [p. 12.28]
9. *F* [p. 12.31]
0. *F* [p. 12.35]

Multiple Choice

1. *c* [p. 12.3]
2. *a* [p. 12.5]
3. *d* [p. 12.9]
4. *d* [p. 12.12]
5. *a* [p. 12.16]
6. *b* [p. 12.19]
7. *b* [p. 12.23]
8. *d* [p. 12.26]
9. *c* [p. 12.30]
0. *b* [p. 12.35]

Fill in the Blanks

1. *comment symbols* or *annotation symbols* [p. 12.10]
2. *flowcharting software* [p. 12.10]
3. *indentation* [p. 12.11]
4. *bugs* [p. 12.14]
5. *implemented* [p. 12.15]
6. *symbolic addresses* [p. 12.17]
7. *macros* [p. 12.17]
8. *query language* [p. 12.18]
9. *information hiding* [p. 12.20]
0. *empower* [p. 12.27]

Complete the Table

STANDARD SYMBOLS USED TO CREATE PROGRAM FLOWCHARTS

Symbol	Operation	Purpose
▭	*PROCESS*	Program instruction(s) that transforms input(s) into output(s)
▱	INPUT/OUTPUT	*Enter data or display information*
◇	*DECISION*	Condition that determines a specified path to follow
⬭	TERMINAL	*Beginning or end of program*

Symbol	Operation	Purpose
◯	*CONNECTOR*	Entry from or exit to another part of the flowchart on the same page
▯	*PREDEFINED PROCESS*	Named process containing a series of specified program steps

Things to Think About

Answers will vary.

Puzzle Answer

1.	set of instructions that directs the computer to perform tasks to process data into information	*computer program* EJGCWMZD CDJUDHG
2.	identifies the inputs to a program, the outputs generated, and the processing steps required	*defining diagram* IZOSBSBU ISHUDHG
3.	used by programmers to represent program modules graphically	*top-down chart* MJC-IJRB EYHDM
4.	graphical or written description of the step-by-step procedures for a module	*program logic* CDJUDHG VJUSE
5.	design that controls the logical order in which program instructions are executed	*construct* EJBQMDWEM
6.	type of control structure that shows a single action, or a single action followed by another action	*sequence* QZXWZBEZ
7.	type of control structure used when an action is to be repeated as long as a certain condition is met	*iteration* SMZDHMSJB
8.	what Nassi-Schneiderman (N-S) charts sometimes are called	*structured flowcharts* QMDWEMWDZI OVJREYHDMQ
9.	documentation within a program	*remarks* DZGHDFQ
10.	allows you to identify syntax errors and find logic errors while a program runs in slow motion	*debugger* IZAWUUZD
11.	error found in many computers at the turn of the century	*Y2k Bug* P2F AWU
12.	meaningful abbreviations for assembly language program instructions	*mnemonics* GBZGJBSEQ

13. software that enables a developer to design or layout a report on the screen — *report generator*
DZCJDM UZBZDHMJD

14. in the object-oriented approach, the procedures in an object — *operations*
JCZDHMSJBQ

15. in the object-oriented approach, the data elements in an object — *variables*
KHDSHAVZQ

16. development tool that allows you to build an application without writing extensive code — *program generator*
CDJUDHG UZBZDHMJD

17. HTML codes that specify links to other documents and how a Web page displays — *markups*
GHDFWCQ

18. collects data from visitors to a Web site, who fill in blank fields — *processing form*
CDJEZQQSBU OJDG

19. simple, open scripting language that anyone can use without purchasing a license — *JavaScript*
THKHQEDSCM

20. Web page development language that some experts predict will replace HTML — *eXtensible Markup*
ZLMZBQSAVZ GHDFWC

To lure expert programmers, in addition to high salaries and
MJ VWDZ ZLCZDM CDJUDHGGZDQ, SB HIISMSJB MJ YSUY QHVHDSZQ HBI

signing bonuses some companies are offering such perks as
QSUBSBU AJBWQZQ QJGZ EJGCHBSZQ HDZ JOOZDSBU QWEY CZDFQ HQ

flexible hours, day care, family leave, stock options, workplace
OVZLSAVZ YJWDQ, IHP EHDZ, OHGSVP VZHKZ, QMJEF JCMSJBQ, RJDFCVHEZ

fitness centers, and even subsidized laundry service.
OSMBZQQ EZBMZDQ, HBI ZKZB QWAQSISNZI VHWBIDP QZDKSEZ.

DISCOVERING COMPUTERS 2000

STUDY GUIDE

CHAPTER 13

Multimedia

Chapter Overview

This chapter explains multimedia, an increasingly important part of business, industry, entertainment, and education. Multimedia is defined and the various media elements – text, graphics, animation, audio, video, and links – are described. You discover how multimedia applications are used in business presentations, computer-based training, Web-based training and distance learning, education, electronic books, electronic references, how-to guides, newspapers and magazines, entertainment and edutainment, virtual reality, kiosks, and the World Wide Web. Multimedia hardware is characterized, including multimedia personal computers, television, data projectors, video capture cards, scanners, digital cameras, photoCDs, laser disks, and laser disk players. Finally, you explore developing multimedia applications, investigating phases in the development process (analysis, design, and production) and multimedia authoring software.

Chapter Objectives

After completing this chapter, you should be able to:

- Define multimedia
- Describe types of media used in multimedia applications
- List and describe the various uses of multimedia applications
- Identify types of multimedia hardware
- Explain how to develop a multimedia application
- Identify features of several multimedia authoring software packages

Chapter Outline

I. What is multimedia? [p. 13.2]

Multimedia refers to ______________________________

____

____

- Interactive multimedia describes ______________________________

  ____

Most interactive multimedia applications allow you to move through materials at your own pace. The ability for users to interact with a multimedia application is one of its more unique and important features.

A. Text [p. 13.3]

Text ____________________

____

B. Graphics [p. 13.3]

A graphic is ____________________

____

Functions of graphics in multimedia applications:

- ____________________
- ____________________
- ____________________

Graphics can be obtained ____________________

____

C. Animation [p. 13.4]

Animation is ____________________

____

D. Audio [p. 13.5]

Audio is ____________________

To store audio, a computer converts analog sound waves into a digital format.

Audio can be obtained ____________________

____

E. Video [p. 13.6]

Video consists of ____________________

____

Like audio files, video files require tremendous amounts of storage space.

Video compression works by ____________________

____

The Moving Pictures Experts Group has ____________________

____

F. Links [p. 13.7]

With many multimedia applications, you can navigate through the content by clicking links.

A link allows users to ____________________

____

II. Multimedia applications [p. 13.8]

A multimedia application involves ______________________________

____

Simulations are ______________________________

____

A. Business presentations [p. 13.8]

Many businesses and industries use multimedia to ______________________________

____

Users can deliver multimedia presentations to large audiences by connecting their computer to a video projector that displays the presentation on a screen.

B. Computer-based training [p. 13.9]

Computer-based training (CBT) is ______________________________

____

Courseware is ______________________________

Advantages of CBT over traditional training:

- ______________ • ______________
- ______________ • ______________
- ______________ • ______________

C. Web-based training (WBT) and distance learning [p. 13.10]

Web-based training (WBT) is ______________________________

____

Distance learning is ______________________________

____

Many colleges and universities offer numerous distance learning courses.

D. Classroom and special education [p. 13.12]

Research has shown that ______________________________

____

Multimedia applications are well suited for ______________________________

____

E. Electronic books [p. 13.13]

One type of electronic book is ______________________________

____

An e-book uses ______________________________

____

F. Electronic reference [p. 13.13]
An electronic reference text is ______________________________

____

G. How-to guides [p. 13.14]
How-to guides are ______________________________

____

H. Newspapers and magazines [p. 13.14]
A multimedia newspaper is ______________________________

____

A multimedia magazine is ______________________________

____

Unlike printed publications, multimedia newspapers and magazines use _____

____

I. Entertainment and edutainment [p. 13.16]
Multimedia computer games ______________________________

____

Edutainment is ______________________________

____

J. Virtual reality [p. 13.16]
Virtual reality (VR) is ______________________________

____

VR is used ______________________________

____

K. Kiosks [p. 13.19]
A kiosk is ______________________________

____

Kiosks often provide information in public places where people have common questions.

L. The World Wide Web [p. 13.19]
The World Wide Web is ______________________________

____

III. Multimedia hardware [p. 13.20]
Hardware selection is an important process in the development and delivery of multimedia products.

A. Multimedia personal computer [p. 13.20]

A multimedia personal computer (MPC) is ______________________________

____

PC 97 is ____

To be considered a PC 97 computer, it must include ____________________

____

MPC components:

1. Sound card [p. 13.21]

   A sound card is ____

   ____

   Typical sound card components:

   - An audio digitizer is ____

     ____

   - The wavetable synthesizer has ________________________________

     ____

   - The mixer combines ____

     ____

2. CD-ROM and DVD-ROM drives [p. 13.21]

   A compact disc is ____

   ____

   Two basic types of compact discs, CD-ROM and DVD-ROM, have large storage capacities that make them excellent media for storing and distributing multimedia applications.

3. Speakers [p. 13.22]

   Small stereo speakers provide _____________________________________

   ____

4. Display device [p. 13.22]

   The display device is ____

   ____

B. Televisions and data projectors [p. 13.22]

Multimedia presentations can be delivered to an audience using a large-screen television or HDTV, or a data projector.

An NTSC converter converts ____

____

A data projector is ____

____

Types of data projectors:

- An LCD projector attaches ____________________
  ____
- A digital light processing (DLP) projector uses ____________________
  ____

C. Video capture card [p. 13.23]

A video capture card is ____________________

____

Video capture software ____________________

____

D. Scanners, digital cameras, and photoCDs [p. 13.23]

To add color images and photographs to multimedia applications, developers can use:

- A color scanner ____________________
  ____
- Digital cameras ____________________
  ____
- A PhotoCD ____________________
  ____

E. Laser disks and laser disk players [p. 13.25]

Laser disks and laser disk players are ____________________

____

IV. Developing multimedia applications [p. 13.25]

Developing multimedia applications follows a standard process with several phases. Activities completed within each phase closely follow those of the PDLC.

A. Analysis [p. 13.26]

____

____

B. Design [p. 13.26]

____

____

The project script provides ____________________

____

C. Production [p. 13.26]

____

____

D. Multimedia authoring software [p. 13.27]

Multimedia authoring software allows ______________________________

____

Factors to consider when selecting a multimedia authoring software package:

- ______________________________
- ______________________________
- ______________________________
- ______________________________
- ______________________________
- ______________________________
- ______________________________

Popular authoring packages:

1. ToolBook [p. 13.27]

   ToolBook ______________________________

   ____

   ToolBook uses a book metaphor ______________________________

   ____

2. Authorware [p. 13.28]

   Authorware ______________________________

   ____

   Authorware uses a flowchart metaphor ______________________________

   ____

3. Director [p. 13.28]

   Director ______________________________

   ____

   Director uses a theater, or movie production, metaphor ______________

   ____

   - The Cast window ______________________________

     ____

   - The Score window ______________________________

     ____

   - The Paint window ______________________________

     ____

Self Test

Matching

1. ____ computer-based training (CBT)
2. ____ Web-based training (WBT)
3. ____ electronic book
4. ____ electronic reference
5. ____ how-to guide
6. ____ multimedia magazine
7. ____ edutainment
8. ____ virtual reality (VR)
9. ____ kiosks
10. ____ the World Wide Web

a. works similarly to a regular camera, but uses a small, reusable disk
b. teaches practical new skills using step-by-step instructions and interactive demonstrations
c. part of the Internet in which multimedia plays an important role
d. digital text that uses links to give the user access to information
e. multimedia experience meant to be both educational and entertaining
f. type of education in which students learn by doing exercises with instructional software
g. digital version of a periodical distributed on CD-ROM or DVD-ROM
h. information source that uses multimedia elements to provide additional information
i. digital version of a magazine created specifically for distribution via the Web
j. approach to CBT that employs technologies of the Internet and World Wide Web
k. computerized information or reference centers used where people have common questions
l. use of computers to create an artificial environment that appears and feels real

True/False

____ 1. Few interactive multimedia applications allow you to move through the materials at your own pace.

____ 2. A video decoder card is less effective and efficient than decompression software.

____ 3. Computer-based training provides a common learning experience because learners receive delayed feedback in the form of additional information for correct answers or actions and negative responses for incorrect answers.

____ 4. Interactive multimedia applications engage students by asking them to define their own paths through an application, which often lead them to explore many related topics.

____ 5. Like printed publications, multimedia magazines and newspapers only use two types of media to convey information.

____ 6. Telecommunications firms and others are using personal computer-based virtual reality (VR) applications for employee training.

____ 7. Most CD-ROM and DVD-ROM drives sold today are external; that is, they are installed outside the system unit of the personal computer.

____ 8. Most DLP projectors require an NTSC converter, while LCD projectors can display SVGA output directly from the computer.

____ 9. As the costs of DVD players continue to drop, experts predict that eventually they will replace laser disk players.

____ 10. Most of today's popular multimedia authoring packages share similar features and are capable of creating similar applications; the major differences exist in the ease of use for development.

Multiple Choice

____ 1. For what type of learners do graphics play an important role in the learning process?
   a. audio learners
   b. visual learners
   c. tactile learners
   d. conceptual learners

____ 2. How does video compression work?
   a. each frame is stored as a separate, smaller file along with an index file that can be used to re-sequence the frames
   b. the first frame is stored and then only pre-selected frames (such as every third frame) are stored
   c. instead of the original frames, a less-detailed, more storage-efficient version of each frame is stored
   d. a first reference frame is stored and then, assuming the following frames will be almost the same, only the changes are stored

____ 3. Which of the following is *not* an advantage of CBT over traditional training?
   a. always up-to-date content
   b. self-paced study
   c. reduced training time
   d. unique instructional experience

____ 4. How much can an e-book hold?
   a. up to 40 pages or about 1 book's worth of text and small graphics
   b. up to 400 pages or about 5 books' worth of text and small graphics
   c. up to 4,000 pages or about 10 books' worth of text and small graphics
   d. up to 40,000 pages or about 50 books' worth of text and small graphics

____ 5. What is Microsoft Encarta?
   a. a popular how-to guide
   b. a popular multimedia magazine
   c. a popular electronic reference
   d. a popular distance learning course

____ 6. In more advanced forms, what does VR software require you to wear?
   a. specialized headgear
   b. body suits
   c. gloves
   d. all of the above

____ 7. When buying a multimedia personal computer, what is the most important consideration for CD-ROM and DVD-ROM drives?
   a. size
   b. speed
   c. accessibility
   d. cost

____ 8. To display multimedia applications effectively, what should your system have?
   a. an MDA monitor with a video card that can display a resolution of 720 x 350
   b. a VGA monitor with a video card that can display a resolution of 640 x 480
   c. an XGA monitor with a video card that can display a resolution of 1024 x 768
   d. an SVGA monitor with a video card that can display a resolution of 800 x 600

____ 9. Once basic requirements for a multimedia application have been determined, what phase begins?
   a. analysis
   b. design
   c. production
   d. test

____ 10. With what multimedia authoring software package do you begin by creating a series of pages, and then add objects such as text fields, buttons, and graphics to each page?
   a. ToolBook
   b. Authorware
   c. Director
   d. PenFold

Fill in the Blanks

1. Instead of using software to decompress a video, some computers include a(n) ____________________, which is an expansion card whose function is to decompress video data.
2. ____________________ compression methods can reduce the size of video files up to 95 percent.
3. Computer-based training, also called ____________________, is popular in business, industry, and schools to teach new skills or enhance existing skills.

4. Interactive CBT software called ____________________ usually is available on CD-ROM or DVD-ROM or shared over a network.
5. ____________________ is the delivery of education at one location while the learning takes place at other locations.
6. A(n) ____________________ is a multimedia magazine created specifically for distribution via the Web.
7. For authoring multimedia applications, you should consider a computer with a 450 MHz ____________________ and 128 MB RAM.
8. NTSC stands for ____________________, which is the organization that sets the standards for most video and broadcast television equipment.
9. Intel's proprietary ____________________ compression technology is used by many manufacturers of video capture cards.
10. Director's programming language, ____________________, can be used to add interactive elements to a multimedia application.

Complete the Table

MULTIMEDIA DEVELOPMENT GUIDELINES

FACTOR	ACTIVITY
________________	Include a self-assessment test to gauge learner needs.
Give the user control	____________________
________________	Use left and right arrows for sequential pages, a stop sign for exit, and so on.
Immerse the user	____________________
________________	Ask questions and provide feedback.
Review concepts	____________________
________________	Make the program attractive and appealing to the eye and ear.
Test the program	____________________

Things to Think About

1. If you were creating a multimedia application describing your college experience, how would you use each media element (text, graphics, animation, audio, video, and links)? Which element would be most important? Why?

2. What advantages that CBT has over traditional training are most important? On what factors might your answer depend? What could be some disadvantages of CBT?
3. What multimedia applications have the greatest impact today? Why? What multimedia applications might have the greatest impact in the future? Why?
4. What multimedia authoring software package – ToolBook, Authorware, or Director – would you most like to use? Why?

Puzzle

All of the words described below appear in the puzzle. Words may be either forward or backward, across, up and down, or diagonal. Circle each word as you find it.

Multimedia

```
              W N S T P
          A G E T A N Y R
        R K R R N     O M O
      D O D A O I       I U D
    G O T H P C A         T L U
    B L C I H S P         X A T C A S T
  E I W E V I R T U A L R E A L I T Y E G
  N O M J D C O T O H P N T V O U M I X E R
K L P R O J E C T S C R I P T I P M E O N A
F C O U R S E W A R E T A E H T D P I D N H
T C O M P A C T D I S C S R E K A E P S I K
B G P J A N I M A T I O N M X E U G O H I A
C E D U T A I N M E N T D R A C D N U O S
    E M A X                   L I Z S
      X D                       O K
```

any computer-based presentation or application that integrates multiple media elements

characters used to create words, sentences, and paragraphs

digital representation of nontext information

graphic that has the illusion of motion

music, speech, or any other sound

photographic images played back at speeds that provide the appearance of full motion

popular standard for video compression and decompression

allows users to navigate from one topic to another in a nonlinear fashion

computer-based models of real-life situations

type of education in which students learn by using and completing exercises with instructional software

interactive CBT software usually available on CD-ROM or DVD-ROM

experience meant to be both educational and entertaining

use of a computer to create an artificial environment that appears and feels real

computerized information reference center that often uses a touch screen

computer that uses specific hardware and software components to input, process, and output various types of multimedia

expansion card that provides both audio input and output

sound card component that combines two signals along with mixing audio

optical storage medium that can hold a tremendous amount of data

provide an easy and inexpensive way to play audio on a multimedia personal computer

uses its own light source to display a multimedia application onto a screen

Intel's proprietary compression technology

in design, provides more detailed information to supplement the flowchart

actual process of creating the various media elements used in a multimedia application and putting them together

metaphor used by ToolBook

metaphor used by Authorware

metaphor used by Director

Director window that serves as a database of various media

Director window used to create animations, synchronize media elements, and control transitions

Director window that contains a drawing and painting program for creating graphics

Self Test Answers

Matching

1. *f* [p. 13.9]
2. *j* [p. 13.10]
3. *d* [p. 13.13]
4. *h* [p. 13.13]
5. *b* [p. 13.14]
6. *g* [p. 13.14]
7. *e* [p. 13.16]
8. *l* [p. 13.16]
9. *k* [p. 13.19]
0. *c* [p. 13.19]

True/False

1. *F* [p. 13.2]
2. *F* [p. 13.6]
3. *F* [p. 13.9]
4. *T* [p. 13.12]
5. *F* [p. 13.14]
6. *T* [p. 13.18]
7. *F* [p. 13.21]
8. *F* [p. 13.23]
9. *T* [p. 13.25]
0. *T* [p. 13.27]

Multiple Choice

1. *b* [p. 13.3]
2. *d* [p. 13.6]
3. *a* [p. 13.10]
4. *c* [p. 13.13]
5. *c* [p. 13.13]
6. *d* [p. 13.17]
7. *b* [p. 13.21]
8. *d* [p. 13.22]
9. *b* [p. 13.26]
0. *a* [p. 13.28]

Fill in the Blanks

1. *video decoder* [p. 13.6]
2. *MPEG* [p. 13.7]
3. *computer-aided instruction (CAI)* [p. 13.9]
4. *courseware* [p. 13.9]
5. *Distance learning* or *Distance education* [p. 13.10]
6. *electronic magazine* or *e-zine* [p. 13.14]
7. *Pentium® III processor* [p. 13.20]
8. *National Television System Committee* [p. 13.22]
9. *digital video interleave (DVI)* [p. 13.23]
0. *Lingo* [p. 13.29]

Complete the Table

MULTIMEDIA DEVELOPMENT GUIDELINES

FACTOR	ACTIVITY
Know your audience	Include a self-assessment test to gauge learner needs.
Give the user control	*Provide a means for the user to navigate his or her own course.*
Use icons with clear meanings	Use left and right arrows for sequential pages, a stop sign for exit, and so on.

FACTOR	ACTIVITY
Immerse the user	*Recreate the tasks users have to perform.*
Require interaction	Ask questions and provide feedback.
Review concepts	*Use self-building exercises.*
Engage the user	Make the program attractive and appealing to the eye and ear.
Test the program	*Test on the target platform with a target audience.*

Things to Think About

Answers will vary.

Puzzle Answer

Multimedia

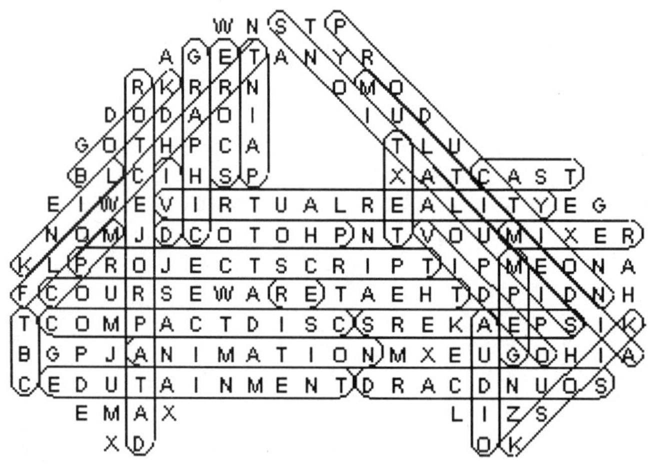

DISCOVERING COMPUTERS 2000

STUDY GUIDE

CHAPTER 14

Security, Privacy, and Ethics

Chapter Overview

This chapter investigates four controversial areas of computer use. First, computer risks and safeguards are examined, including computer viruses, virus detection and removal, unauthorized access and use, hardware theft, software theft, information theft, system failure, backup procedures, disaster recovery plans, and computer security plans. You then study issues related to information privacy, such as unauthorized collection and use of information and employee monitoring. Concerns regarding ethics in the information age, including information accuracy and codes of conduct, are presented. Finally, you consider Internet security and privacy issues such as Internet encryption and objectionable materials on the Internet.

Chapter Objectives

After completing this chapter, you should be able to:

- Identify the various types of security risks that can threaten computers
- Describe ways to safeguard a computer
- Describe how a computer virus works and the steps individuals can take to prevent viruses
- Explain why computer backup is important and how it is accomplished
- Discuss the steps in a disaster recovery plan
- Examine the issues relating to information privacy
- Discuss ethical issues with respect to the information age
- Identify and explain Internet-related security and privacy issues

Chapter Outline

I. Computer security: Risks and safeguards [p. 14.2]

A computer security risk is ______________________________

____

A computer crime is ______________________________

____

Safeguards are ______________________________

A. Computer viruses [p. 14.2]

A computer virus is ______________________________

____

Currently, more than 13,000 known virus programs exist.

Types of viruses:

- A boot sector virus replaces ______________________________

  ____

- A file virus attaches ______________________________

  ____

- A Trojan horse virus is ______________________________

  ____

- A macro virus uses ______________________________

  ____

Triggering a virus:

- A logic bomb is ______________________________
- A time bomb is ______________________________

A worm program copies ______________________________

____

B. Virus detection and removal [p. 14.4]

An antivirus program protects ______________________________

____

- A virus signature is ______________________________

  ____

  A polymorphic virus is difficult to detect because ______________________________

  ____

- To inoculate a program file, the antivirus program records ______________________________

  ____

  A stealth virus can ______________________________

  ____

- When you quarantine a file ______________________________

  ____

- A rescue disk is ______________________________

  ____

C. Unauthorized access and use [p. 14.6]

Unauthorized access is ______________________________

____

- A cracker or hacker is ____

____

Unauthorized use is ____

____

An access control is ____

____

Access controls often are implemented using a two-phase process:

- Identification ____
- Authentication ____

Methods of identification and authorization:

1. User identification and passwords [p. 14.6]

   With a user identification and password, you are required to ____________

   ____

2. Possessed objects [p. 14.7]

   A possessed object is ____

   ____

   A personal identification number (PIN) is ______________________

   ____

3. Biometric devices [p. 14.8]

   A biometric device authenticates ______________________________

   ____

   Types of biometric devices:

   - Fingerprint scanners ______________________________________
   - Hand geometry systems ____________________________________
   - Biometric pens ____
   - Keystroke analysis devices ________________________________
   - Retinal scanners ____

4. Callback system [p. 14.8]

   With a callback system, you ________________________________

   ____

   An audit trail or log records ________________________________

   ____

D. Hardware theft [p. 14.9]

Hardware theft ____

To minimize hardware theft ______________________________

____

____

Computer vandalism ______________________________

E. Software theft [p. 14.10]

Software theft ______________________________

____

Software piracy is ______________________________

____

A software license is ______________________________

____

A single-user license typically includes the following conditions:

- ______________________________
- ______________________________
- ______________________________
- ______________________________

The Business Software Alliance (BSA) ______________________________

____

To reduce software costs, organizations can obtain:

- A site license ______________________________
- A network site license ______________________________

F. Information theft [p. 14.12]

Information theft ______________________________

____

Information theft usually is prevented by implementing user identification and authentication controls. One way to protect data on a network is to encrypt it.

1. Encryption [p. 14.12]

   Encryption is ______________________________

   ____

   - Plaintext ______________________________
   - Ciphertext ______________________________
   - An encryption key ______________________________

   Types of encryption:

   - Private key encryption ______________________________

     ____

     Data encryption standard (DES) ______________________________

- Public key encryption ______________________________

  ____

  RSA ______________________________

G. System failure [p. 14.14]

A system failure is ______________________________

____

Electrical disturbances:

- Noise ______________________________
- Undervoltage ______________________________

  A brownout ______________________________

  A blackout ______________________________
- Overvoltage ______________________________

  A spike ______________________________

A surge protector uses ______________________________

____

Surge protectors should meet specifications of the Underwriters Laboratories (UL) 1449 standard and have a Joule (the amount of energy that can be absorbed before damage occurs) rating of at least 200.

An uninterruptable power supply (UPS) connects ______________________________

____

- A standby UPS ______________________________
- An online UPS ______________________________

H. Backup procedures [p. 14.16]

A backup is ______________________________

____

Types of backup:

- A full backup ______________________________
- A differential backup ______________________________
- An incremental backup ______________________________

Backup procedures specify ______________________________

____

A three-generation backup policy ______________________________

____

I. Disaster recovery plan [p. 14.18]

A disaster recovery plan is ______________________________

____

Disaster recovery plan components:

1. The emergency plan [p. 14.18]
   An emergency plan specifies ________________________________

   ____
2. The backup plan [p. 14.18]
   The backup plan specifies ________________________________

   ____
3. The recovery plan [p. 14.18]
   The recovery plan specifies ________________________________

   ____
4. The test plan [p. 14.19]
   The test plan contains ________________________________

   ____

J. Developing a computer security plan [p. 14.19]

A computer security plan summarizes ________________________________

____

A computer security plan should:

____

____

____

II. Information privacy [p. 14.20]

Information privacy refers to ________________________________

____

A. Unauthorized collection and use of information [p. 14.20]

____

____

Common points in laws regarding the storage and use of personal data:

(1) ____

(2) ____

(3) ____

(4) ____

Federal laws dealing specifically with computers:

- Electronic Communications Privacy Act (ECPA) ____________________

  ____

- Computer Matching and Privacy Protection Act ______________________________
- Computer Fraud and Abuse Acts ______________________________
- Fair Credit Reporting Act ______________________________

B. Employee monitoring [p. 14.22]
Employee monitoring involves ______________________________

The proposed Privacy for Consumers and Workers Act states that ______________________________

III. Ethics and the information age [p. 14.23]
Computer ethics are ______________________________

Areas of computer ethics: unauthorized use, software theft, information privacy, information accuracy, and codes of ethical conduct.

A. Information accuracy [p. 14.23]
Information accuracy is ______________________________

B. Codes of conduct [p. 14.24]
Codes of conduct are ______________________________

IV. Internet security and privacy issues [p. 14.25]
On a vast network such as the Internet with no central administrator, security risks are great; every computer along the route data takes can look at what is being sent or received.

A. Internet encryption [p. 14.25]
To provide secure data transmission, many browsers use encryption.
Popular uses of encryption on the Internet:

1. Secure Sockets Layer [p. 14.26]
Secure Sockets Layer (SSL) provides ______________________________

Secure servers are ______________________________

2. Digital signatures [p. 14.26]

   A digital signature is ____

   ____

   A digital signature is a type of digital certificate.

   A digital certificate is ____

   A certificate authority (CA) is ____

   ____

B. Objectionable materials on the Internet [p. 14.27]

   The most discussed ethical issue concerning the Internet is ______________

   ____

   The Communications Decency Act ____

   ____

   One approach to restricting access is ____

   ____

Self Test

Matching

1. ____ boot sector virus
2. ____ file virus
3. ____ Trojan horse virus
4. ____ macro virus
5. ____ logic bomb
6. ____ time bomb
7. ____ worm
8. ____ antivirus program
9. ____ polymorphic virus
10. ____ stealth virus

a. identifies and removes any viruses in memory or on a storage media
b. infects a program file but still reports the size and creation date of the uninfected program
c. duplicates all of the program and data files in the computer
d. copies itself repeatedly in memory or on a disk drive until no memory or disk space remains
e. replaces the program used to start a computer with an infected version
f. converts readable data into unreadable characters to prevent unauthorized access
g. uses the macro language of an application to hide virus code
h. activates on a particular date
i. modifies its program code each time it attaches itself to another program or file
j. attaches itself to program files and spreads to any file that accesses the infected program
k. activates when it detects a certain condition
l. hides within or is designed to look like a legitimate program

True/False

____ 1. The increased use of networks, the Internet, and e-mail has accelerated the spread of computer viruses by allowing individuals to share files more easily.

____ 2. Completely effective methods exist to ensure that a computer or network is safe from computer viruses.

____ 3. Callback systems work best for users who work primarily at different remote sites or locations that vary unpredictably from one day to the next.

____ 4. Site license fees usually cost significantly less than purchasing individual copies of software for each computer at a single location.

____ 5. The lower the Joule rating of a surge protector, the better the protection.

____ 6. Generally, an organization develops backup procedures in which a differential or incremental backup is performed at regular intervals, and full backups are performed between each differential or incremental backup.

____ 7. A computer security plan should identify all information assets, identify security risks, and, for each risk, identify the safeguards that exist to detect, prevent, and recover from a loss.

____ 8. Most organizations have formal e-mail policies, which mean, in effect, that e-mail cannot be read without employee notification.

____ 9. Information transmitted over networks has a higher degree of security risk than information kept on an organization's premises.

____ 10. Web pages that use SSL typically begin with the https protocol, instead of the http protocol.

Multiple Choice

____ 1. What type of virus often is hidden in templates so that it will infect any document using the template?
   a. boot sector virus
   b. file virus
   c. Trojan horse virus
   d. macro virus

____ 2. Which of the following is *not* a criteria to be guided by when creating a password?
   a. make the password at least eight characters long
   b. mix initials and dates together
   c. choose names of familiar places in your native country
   d. join two words together

____ 3. Why are biometric devices gaining popularity as a security precaution?
   a. they are a virtually foolproof method of identification
   b. they are unaffected by physical conditions or feelings of stress
   c. they are less expensive than other forms of identification
   d. all of the above

____ 4. Which of the following is *not* a condition typically included in a single-user license agreement?
   a. users can install the software on only *one* computer
   b. users can install the software on a network
   c. users can make *one* copy for backup purposes
   d. users cannot give copies to friends and colleagues

____ 5. Why is software piracy a serious offense?
   a. it increases the chance of viruses
   b. it reduces your ability to receive technical support
   c. it drives up the price of software for all users
   d. all of the above

____ 6. What type of backup provides the best protection against data loss but can take a long time?
   a. full backup
   b. partial backup
   c. differential backup
   d. incremental backup

____ 7. In a three-generation backup, what are the oldest copy, second oldest copy, and most recent copy of the file called?
a. child, parent, grandparent
b. grandparent, parent, child
c. child, grandparent, parent
d. parent, grandparent, child

____ 8. What disaster recovery plan component should contain names and telephone numbers of people and organizations to be notified, equipment procedures to be followed, evacuation procedures, and return procedures?
a. the emergency plan
b. the backup plan
c. the recovery plan
d. the test plan

____ 9. Which of the following is *not* a common point in laws regarding the storage and disclosure of personal data?
a. information collected and stored should be limited to what is necessary to carry out the function of the collecting business or government agency
b. once collected, access should be restricted to employees within the organization who need access to it to perform their jobs
c. personal information can be released outside the organization collecting the data regardless of whether or not the person has agreed to its release
d. an individual should know the data is being collected and have the opportunity to determine the accuracy of the data

____ 10. How do Secure Sockets Layer (SSL) and digital signatures (or digital IDs) encrypt data and signatures?
a. both SSL and digital IDs use a private key
b. SSL uses a private key and digital IDs use a public key
c. both SSL and digital IDs use a public key
d. SSL uses a public key and digital IDs use a private key

Fill in the Blanks

1. A(n) ____________________ is any event or action that could cause damage to computer hardware, software, data, information, or processing capability.
2. A rescue disk, or ____________________, is a disk that contains an uninfected copy of key operating system commands and startup information.
3. A computer should record both successful and unsuccessful access attempts in a file called a(n) ____________________.
4. A single-user license, also called a(n) ____________________, is the most common type of license included with software purchased by individual users.
5. To read encrypted data, the recipient must ____________________, or decipher, it into readable form.

6. An overvoltage or ____________________ occurs when the incoming electrical power increases significantly above the normal 120 volts.
7. A surge protector, also called a(n) ____________________, uses special electrical components to smooth out minor noise, provide a stable current flow, and keep an overvoltage from reaching the computer and other electronic equipment.
8. A standby UPS, sometimes called a(n) ____________________, switches to battery power when a problem occurs in the power line.
9. Companies and individuals who need help with computer security plans can contact the ____________________ via the telephone or on the Web for assistance.
10. A(n) ____________________ is a notice that guarantees a user or a Web site is legitimate.

Complete the Table

MAJOR U.S. GOVERNMENT LAWS CONCERNING PRIVACY

DATE	LAW	PURPOSE
1997	____________________ ____________________	Closed a loophole in the law that allowed people to give away copyrighted material on the Internet.
_____	National Information Infrastructure Protection Act	Penalizes theft of information across state lines, threats against networks, and computer system trespassing.
1994	Computer Abuse Amendments Act	____________________ ____________________
1988	____________________ ____________________	Regulates the use of government data to determine the eligibility of individuals for federal benefits.
_____	Electronic Communications Privacy Act (ECPA)	Provides the established right of privacy protection to new forms of electronic communications.
1984	Computer Fraud and Abuse Act	____________________ ____________________
1974	____________________	Forbids federal agencies from allowing information to be used for a reason other than for which it was collected.
_____	Family Educational Rights and Privacy Act	Gives students and parents access to school records and limits disclosure to unauthorized parties.

Things to Think About

1. Four methods of identification and authentication are user identification and passwords, possessed objects, biometric devices, and callback systems. What are the advantages of each method? What are the disadvantages?
2. In response to the problem of information theft, two government proposals are Clipper chip and the key escrow plan. How are the proposals different? Why do you think each proposal has been opposed?
3. The goal of a computer security plan is to match an appropriate level of safeguards against the identified risks. What is meant by this? How might this goal affect the security plans of an individual, a school, a business, and a government agency?
4. Laws regarding unauthorized collection and use of information, employee monitoring, information accuracy, and objectionable material on the Internet remain incomplete. For which area is the need for legislation most pressing? Why?

Puzzle

Use the given clues to complete the crossword puzzle.

Security, Privacy, and Ethics

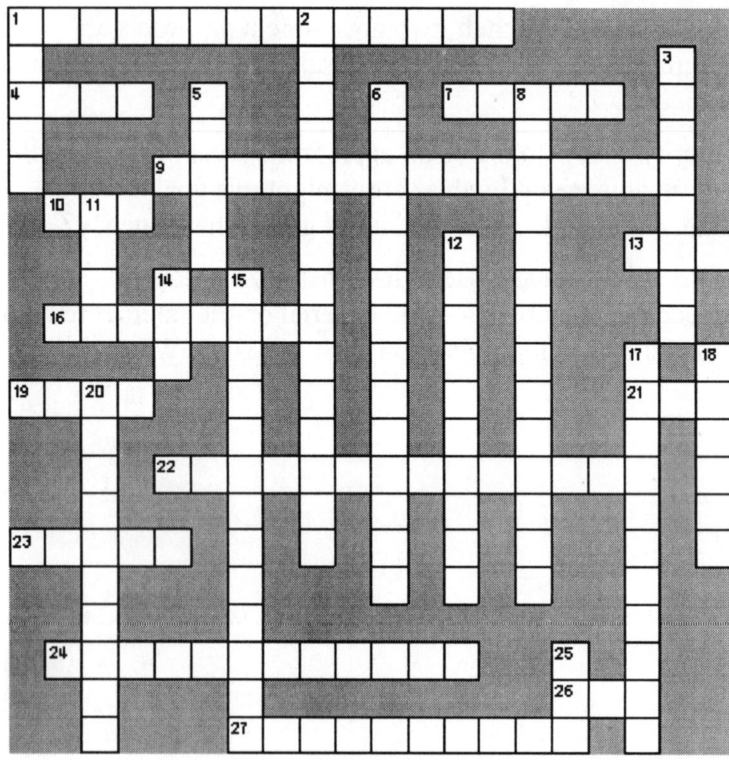

Down

1. Momentary overvoltage
2. Item that must be carried to gain access to a computer or computer facility
3. Type of virus that activates on a particular date
5. Unwanted electrical signal mixed with normal voltage entering the computer
6. Known pattern of virus code
8. Verifies an individual is a valid user
11. Common type of license included with software purchased by individual users
12. Type of virus that replaces the program used to start the computer
14. Formed by a number of software companies to combat piracy
15. Potentially damaging program designed to negatively affect the way a computer works
17. In a three-generation backup plan, the oldest copy of the file
18. Individual who accesses a computer or network illegally
20. Disk that contains an uninfected copy of key operating system commands
25. Uses batteries to provide electricity for a limited amount of time

Across

1. Unauthorized and illegal duplication of copyrighted programs
4. Provides help with computer security plans via telephone or the Web
7. In a three-generation backup plan, the most recent copy of the file
9. Authenticates a person by verifying personal characteristics
10. Most popular private key encryption system
13. File that records both successful and unsuccessful access attempts
16. Series of characters that matches an entry in an authorization file
19. Program that copies itself repeatedly into memory
21. Powerful public key encryption technology
22. Verifies an individual is who he or she claims to be
23. Amount of energy a surge protector can absorb before it is damaged
24. Type of backup that duplicates only files that have changed since the last full backup
26. Numeric password
27. Protective measures taken to minimize security risks

Self Test Answers

Matching

1. *e* [p. 14.3]
2. *j* [p. 14.3]
3. *l* [p. 14.3]
4. *g* [p. 14.3]
5. *k* [p. 14.4]
6. *h* [p. 14.4]
7. *d* [p. 14.4]
8. *a* [p. 14.4]
9. *i* [p. 14.5]
0. *b* [p. 14.5]

True/False

1. *T* [p. 14.3]
2. *F* [p. 14.4]
3. *F* [p. 14.9]
4. *T* [p. 14.12]
5. *F* [p. 14.15]
6. *F* [p. 14.17]
7. *T* [p. 14.19]
8. *F* [p. 14.22]
9. *T* [p. 14.25]
0. *T* [p. 14.26]

Multiple Choice

1. *d* [p. 14.4]
2. *c* [p. 14.6]
3. *a* [p. 14.8]
4. *b* [p. 14.10]
5. *d* [p. 14.11]
6. *a* [p. 14.16]
7. *b* [p. 14.18]
8. *a* [p. 14.18]
9. *c* [p. 14.21]
0. *b* [p. 14.26]

Fill in the Blanks

1. *computer security risk* [p. 14.2]
2. *emergency disk* [p. 14.6]
3. *audit trail* or *log* [p. 14.9]
4. *end-user license agreement (EULA)* [p. 14.10]
5. *decrypt* [p. 14.12]
6. *power surge* [p. 14.15]
7. *surge suppressor* [p. 14.15]
8. *offline UPS* [p. 14.16]
9. *International Computer Security Association (ICSA)* [p. 14.19]
0. *certificate* or *digital certificate* [p. 14.26]

Complete the Table

MAJOR U.S. GOVERNMENT LAWS CONCERNING PRIVACY

DATE	LAW	PURPOSE
1997	*No Electronic Theft (NET) Act*	Closed a loophole in the law that allowed people to give away copyrighted material on the Internet.
1996	National Information Infrastructure Protection Act	Penalizes theft of information across state lines, threats against networks, and computer system trespassing.

DATE	LAW	PURPOSE
1994	Computer Abuse Amendments Act	*Amends 1984 act to outlaw transmission of harmful computer code such as viruses.*
1988	*Computer Matching and Privacy Protection Act*	Regulates the use of government data to determine the eligibility of individuals for federal benefits.
1986	Electronic Communications Privacy Act (ECPA)	Provides the established right of privacy protection to new forms of electronic communications.
1984	Computer Fraud and Abuse Act	*Outlaws unauthorized access of federal government computers.*
1974	*Privacy Act*	Forbids federal agencies from allowing information to be used for a reason other than for which it was collected.
1974	Family Educational Rights and Privacy Act	Gives students and parents access to school records and limits disclosure to unauthorized parties.

Things to Think About

Answers will vary.

Puzzle Answer

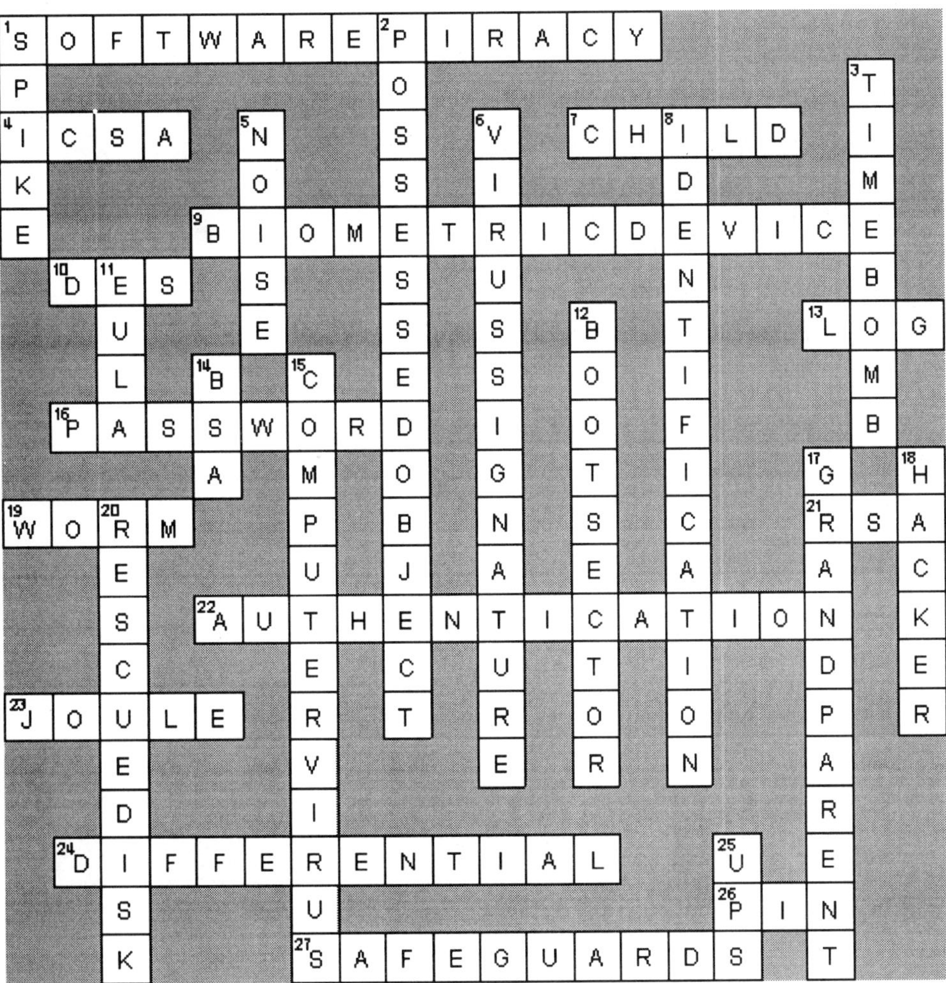